A Bark In Tl

The 45 Best Places To Hike With Your Dog In The El Paso/Las Cruces Region

JESSICA POWERS

illustrations by
ANDREW CHESWORTH

Cruden Bay Books

for Chris and Cooper

A BARK IN THE PARK: THE 45 BEST PLACES TO HIKE
WITH YOUR DOG IN THE EL PASO/LAS CRUCES
REGION

Cruden Bay Books
PO Box 467
Montchanin, DE 19710

www.hikewithyourdog.com

International Standard Book Number 0-9644427-6-0

Manufactured in the United States of America

"Dogs are our link to paradise...to sit with a dog on a hillside on a glorious afternoon is to be back in Eden, where doing nothing was not boring - it was peace."

- Milan Kundera

Contents

Introduction

A few months ago, my husband Chris and my dad were visiting Albuquerque, New Mexico, the city where I lived for the first eight years of my life. As they drove into the Sandia Mountains, Dad told Chris that when he started agitating to take us kids hiking, he and my mother devised a rule: they wouldn't take us on really long hikes until we were at least six, old enough to handle the distance. "Jessica broke that rule!" Dad told Chris.

When I was just four, Dad and I hiked from the foothills of the Sandia Mountains to Sandia Peak and then down the other side of the mountain to Aunt Sandy and Uncle Al's house on the other side of the mountain. I remember vividly my mother dropping Dad and me off in the foothills of the Sandia Mountains and watching for the little splotches of orange paint that marked the trail. I remember stopping along the way to eat my mother's oatmeal chocolate chip cookies and drinking chicken bouillon at the top of the Sandias, among the pine trees, my dad having boiled the water on a tiny gas burner.

Dad was a geologist, so my brothers and I grew up camping and hiking in such cool places as the Badlands of South Dakota and Wyoming, hunting for fossils. We found something once, some pig's teeth, which Dad left for a scientist he knew at a museum. The lady at the museum gave me a small pink plastic purse with fake little girl lipsticks in exchange for the fossils. It didn't seem like a fair exchange to me.

We never took our dogs hiking. On occasion, they'd go on vacations with us, so they'd end up camping with us, but I don't remember any hikes when our dogs were "on the trail" with us.

We grew up as outdoors people, but never the kind of outdoors people that had a lot of money for fancy equipment. Geologists a) never have money, b) make do with what they've got and c) care more about rocks than camping equipment.

Who cares what you must sleep on as long as you can spend all day running around the mountain with little hammers? I'm not making fun; I'm a little jealous, actually.

A few years ago, when I was living in upstate New York and spending most of my time in the library as a graduate student in history, I decided I wanted to move back West, where I'd lived the first twenty-five years of my life. I wanted a dog and a Jeep Cherokee. I wanted to take my dog hiking all the time. I wanted to be one of those cool twenty-some-things who do a lot of rock climbing and have a well-behaved dog and a great SUV and live in Seattle.

I have the dog now - Cooper - but the SUV will have to wait. Cooper, Chris and I head to the hills in our handy-dandy Toyota Tercel. And Cooper is, fortunately, perfectly behaved off the leash! Hence, I'm always glad when I stumble onto BLM managed land and can let Cooper run wild and free. So now we live here in El Paso, Texas - hardly a cool city for young people, but it has its perks, among them the cost of living.

Cooper is, ahem, our child. We literally take him every-where. Chris takes him to work almost every day. We take him hiking on weekends. Cooper, like any typical Yellow Lab under three years old, is either full-blast energy - running and leaping and uncontained (unless restrained by the leash, of course) - or sleeping on our bed, his favorite spot in the house.

I'd like to say that I had a systematic methodology for this book, but mostly, it was a good excuse to let Cooper tire out so he would behave at home. Also, it got me out into this land I love, the Chihuahuan Desert, which seems stark and barren to many people until they've lived here long enough to notice the little beauties along the way. Then I could dig around and find out about the history and geology that makes this place interesting.

One of my ulterior motives in writing this book was introducing Chris to the desert. Chris grew up in Massachusetts, then lived the cool twenty-something life in Seattle for four years before he married me. It has taken him a year to adjust to the desert, but he is beginning to see the subtle and stark beauty here, which is very different from the overwhelming, majestic, and very obvious beauty of the Northwest. At risk of alienating my husband, who thinks Seattle has the perfect weather, I think Cooper loves the desert southwest more than the wet northwest. At least, he never wanted to go out when it rained there, which is a problem considering how frequently it rains. He loves water, but not the kind that falls from the sky.

Oh, by the way, Cooper was named for Chris's favorite author, James Fenimore Cooper. Our next pet, when Cooper can handle a sibling, will be a black cat named - you guessed it -Poe.

-Jessica

"Happiness is dog-shaped"
- Chapman Pincher

Preface

The Land. This book is about taking your dog to hike in the desert, a stark land with little vegetation and fewer trees. To really appreciate the beauty of this land, stop looking at the landscape and notice the panorama: strange mountain shapes, layers of rock, plants that survive in the desert, and small creatures busy at work, such as ants carrying the husk of a baby lizard.

This region of the Southwest is dominated by the Rio Grande Rift or the Rio Grande Valley. For thousands of years, American Indians lived here in pueblos or caves, first as hunter-gatherers and then as farmers. In the El Paso region, archeologists believe that the Suma, Manso and Jumano Indians arrived around 1200 B.C. They survived by hunting animals, gathering nuts and berries, and farming. The Rio Grande, then a vast river, sustained these early agricultural efforts, as well as providing fish for the local diet.

Life changed in 1535 with the arrival of Europeans. The Spanish conquistador, Alvar Nuñez Cabeza de Vaca, along with two other Spaniards and the Moorish slave Estebanico, wandered into the region where modern day El Paso and Las Cruces are today. They were traveling to fulfill Cabeza de Vaca's quest to know the land from Florida to the Rio de las Palmas. The travelers carried tales of this land to the Spaniards they met, triggering the conquest of the late sixteenth and seventeenth centuries. In 1598, the Spanish Conquistador Juan de Òate arrived on the banks of the Rio Grande near present-day El Paso, straggling up through the Chihuahua Desert from Mexico City. The Rio Grande was the first water the conquistadors had seen in many days and they went crazy with joy. Two men drank until their bellies burst and they died, while the stream carried two horses away. The American Indians who lived here, the Manso, were friendly, so the Conquistadors sank to their knees in thankfulness and gave a tremendous feast, which, historians have argued, is the very *first* European Thanksgiving on American soil.

The Environment. To understand the geology of the Rio Grande Rift Valley, you must first understand the theory of plate tectonics. According to this theory, the upper part of the earth's crust is broken into twelve large, rigid plates. Several smaller plates are scattered among these twelve large plates. The plates are not stationary; rather, they move slowly about, combining with or breaking apart from other plates. Earthquakes and volcanic activity provide evidence for the movement of the plates.

The North American plate - which stretches from the mid-Atlantic Ridge to the Pacific Coast - has been drifting westward for hundreds of millions of years, widening the Atlantic Ocean. In New Mexico, two parts of the North American plate appear to be separating, creating the Rio Grande Rift Valley. This valley is similar to the Rift Valley in eastern Africa.

As the crust in the North American plate stretched, it thinned and cracked, creating faults. Along these faults, blocks of the earth fell to create a series of valleys and a series of mountain ranges, a topography known as Basin and Range. This topography begins along the Sacramento and Guadalupe Mountains and characterizes much of the West, including southwestern New Mexico, Arizona, and states to the North. The Rio Grande River follows a series of these valleys from Southern Colorado down through El Paso and on southward.

Distance To Drive To These Hikes

From either El Paso or Las Cruces, it takes from 30 minutes to one hour to drive to most of the hikes and parks included in this book. However, because there are so few people in the West, distances can be deceiving. For one thing, the interstate highway system gets you to a hike much faster than driving the same distance in the East or along California's crowded freeways. Yet, at the same time, many of the most solitary hikes in this book (like those on Bureau of Land Management land) are reached via desolate county roads or unimproved dirt roads. Though the distance may be shorter than a hike reached by the interstate, the actual driving time can be longer because of the access roads involved. A variety of hikes within (Western-style) reasonable distances are included. Also, to suggest a few canine hikes in non-desert environments, walks in the Gila (HEE-la) Wilderness and the Lincoln National Forest are in the book.

"What counts is not necessarily the size of the dog in the fight but the size of the fight in the dog."
- Dwight D. Eisenhower

Cautionary Words To Carry Into The Desert

Hiking in southern New Mexico and west Texas means hiking in a desert environment. If you are unused to hiking in general, or used to hiking in mountainous regions or cool climates, you can easily find yourself in trouble unless you heed some simple common-sense precautions.

🐾 Avoid hiking in June or July

The optimum hiking period here is August through May. If you must hike in June and July, stick to the early morning or evening. Daytime heat is blistering, and it is dangerous to be out in direct sun exercising for long hours. Even if *you* can stand the heat, chances are your dog - with no sweat glands and only an inefficient system of panting to disperse body heat - can not. Although desert heat is dry, most of these hikes provide few, if any, trees for shade and little or no water for swimming or drinking. Hiking in this kind of heat may not only give your dog heat stroke, but she may burn the pads on her paws on the hot sand or scorching cement.

🐾 Bring plenty of water, no matter how cold it seems when you set out

The desert is dry, dry, dry, and it is unlikely you will encounter water anywhere along your route. If there are three of us (Cooper, me, and my husband), we carry two gallons of water for a 2-3 hour hike. Sometimes we drink it all, and sometimes we don't, but it is always better in the desert to bring more water than you need. If you have a big dog who drinks more than his share, get him a pack so he can carry his own water.

🐾 Be prepared for varying temperatures

The desert is an environment of extremes, which includes fluctuation in temperature. In the winter, the temperature can dip well below freezing at night, even reaching single-digit temperatures, and then climb to 60 or 70 degrees Farenheit during the day. Summer temperatures can dip to 50 degrees at night, seeming quite cool, and then reach over 100 degrees during the day.

☙ Wear sunscreen and a hat
Always, always.

☙ Avoid arroyos, ditches, and washes when it is raining
Flash floods occur in the desert after significant rainfall.
Water cascades down from the mountains; arroyos that have
been dry for years can fill to the brim within seconds.
Though flash floods are rare, they occur without warning.
Please take this caution seriously. Hiking in arroyos is perfectly
safe when it is not raining, but forego hiking plans if it is,
especially if you see thunderclouds and rain in nearby
mountain ranges. Almost every year, somebody in or around
El Paso dies in a flash flood. El Paso and Las Cruces receive
less than 10 inches of rainfall annually, most of it falling
during the month of August, when the desert monsoons hit.

**☙ Keep an eye out for rattlesnakes, scorpions, centipedes
and black widow spiders**
I make this statement with caution, realizing that some folks
will be scared of hiking in the desert because they are afraid
of snakes. I want to emphasize one point, however: in all the
weeks and months of hiking to research this book, and in all
the years of desert hiking that I did growing up here with a
geologist father, the only snakes, scorpions, or spiders I ever
encountered were in my own backyard.

☙ A word about rattlesnakes
During the months of December, January, and February,
rattlesnakes hibernate so you won't encounter them.
During the summer months, they generally emerge only at
night because they can't regulate their body temperature and
the heat is too intense. During spring and autumn, however,
you may see them during the day. Unless cornered or
teased by humans, a rattlesnake will crawl away and avoid
striking. If you are hiking in remote regions outlined in this
book at any time other than winter, wear protective clothing.
Avoid rocky areas, crevasses, caves, and areas where the
ground cover (weed or grass) prevents you from seeing the
ground. These are all places where snakes are likely to hang
out. Stick to trails and roads. It's always a good idea to buy

a snakebite kit at the local camping or sports store. If you encounter a snake, scold your dog severely (or use whatever method you normally use to train her.) Terry Chandler, a professional snake-avoidance trainer, lives in Las Cruces and will train dogs and horses to stay away from rattlesnakes. It is worth the $50 he charges, especially if you like hiking in the remote places mentioned in this book, because your dogs will be "snake-broke" for life. He can be reached at (505) 382-5231.

🐾 Other animals to watch out for
These include bears (especially in the Lincoln National Forest) and mountain lions. Steve Stochaj, who has worked on the Search and Rescue Team in Las Cruces for seven years, says bears will stay away as long as you make plenty of noise. Mountain lions are usually only a concern at night, but he suggests that you keep your dog close to you since mountain lions are afraid of people but not afraid of dogs.

🐾 Stay away from old mines
As you hike in the mountainous regions, you may encounter old mine shafts. They are fragile, could collapse, and may contain toxic gases.

🐾 Hunting minerals or removing plant species from federally owned land or state parks is prohibited
Although cacti may seem prolific out in the desert, many species are endangered, and thus, protected in their natural environment. Do not remove them. The penalties can be quite severe if you are caught.

Hiking With Your Dog

So you want to start hiking with your dog. Hiking with your dog can be a fascinating way to explore the region around El Paso and Las Cruces from a canine perspective. Some things to consider:

🐾 Dog's Health

Hiking can be a wonderful preventative for any number of physical and behavioral disorders. One in every three dogs is overweight and running up trails and leaping through arroyos is great exercise to help keep pounds off. Hiking can also relieve boredom in a dog's routine and calm dogs prone to destructive habits. And hiking with your dog strengthens the overall owner/dog bond.

🐾 Breed of Dog

All dogs enjoy the new scents and sights of a trail. But some dogs are better suited to hiking than others. If you don't as yet have a hiking companion, select a breed that matches your interests. Do you look forward to an entire afternoon's hiking? You'll need a dog bred to keep up with such a pace, such as a retriever or a spaniel. Is a half-hour enough walking for you? It may not be for an energetic dog like a border collie. If you already have a hiking friend, tailor your plans to his abilities.

🐾 Conditioning

Just like humans, dogs need to be acclimated to the task at hand. An inactive dog cannot be expected to bounce from the easy chair in the den to complete a 3-hour hike. You must also be physically able to restrain your dog if confronted with distractions on the trail (like a scampering squirrel or a pack of joggers). Have your dog checked by a veterinarian before significantly increasing her activity level.

🐾 Weather

Heat and sun do dogs no favors. With no sweat glands and only panting available to disperse body heat, dogs are much more susceptible to heat stroke than we are. Unusually rapid panting and/or a bright red tongue are signs of heat exhaustion in your pet. Always carry enough water for your hike. Even the days that don't seem too warm can cause discomfort in dark-coated dogs if the sun is shining brightly. In cold weather, short-coated breeds may require additional attention.

🐾 Water

Surface water, including fast-flowing streams, is likely to be infested with a microscopic protozoa called *Giardia*, waiting to wreak havoc on a dog's intestinal system. The most common symptom is crippling diarrhea. Algae, pollutants and contaminants can all be in streams, ponds and puddles. If possible, carry fresh water for your dog on the trail - your dog can even learn to drink happily from a squirt bottle.

*"He is very imprudent, a dog is. He never makes it
his business to inquire whether you are in the
right or in the wrong, never bothers
as to whether you are going up or down
upon's life ladder, never asks whether you are
rich or poor, silly or wise, sinner or saint."*
- Jerome K. Jerome

Outfitting Your Dog For A Hike

These are the basics for taking your dog on a hike:

▸ **Collar**. It should not be so loose as to come off but you should be able to slide your flat hand under collar.

▸ **Identification Tags**.

▸ **Bandanna**. Can help distinguish your dog from game in hunting season.

▸ **Leash**. Leather lasts forever but if there's water in your dog's future, consider quick-drying nylon.

🐾 I want my dog to help carry water, snacks and other supplies on the trail. How do I choose a dog pack?
To select an appropriate dog pack, measure your dog's girth around the rib cage to determine the best pack size. A dog pack should fit securely without hindering the dog's ability to walk normally.

🐾 How does a dog wear a pack?
The pack, typically with cargo pouches on either side, should ride as close to the shoulders as possible without limiting movement. The straps that hold the dog pack in place should be situated where they will not cause chafing.

🐾 Will my dog wear a pack?
Wearing a dog pack is no more obtrusive than wearing a collar, although some dogs will take to a pack easier than others. Introduce the pack by draping a towel over your dog's back in the house and then having him wear an empty pack on short walks. Progressively add some crumpled newspaper and then bits of clothing. Fill the pack with treats and reward your dog from the stash. Soon he will associate the dog pack with an outdoor adventure and will eagerly look forward to wearing it.

🐾 How much weight can I put into a dog pack?

Many dog packs are sold by weight recommendations. A healthy, well-conditioned dog can comfortably carry 25% to 33% of its body weight. Breeds prone to back problems or hip dysplasia should not wear dog packs. Consult your veterinarian before stuffing the pouches with gear.

🐾 What are good things to put in a dog pack?

Low density items such as food and poop bags are good choices. Ice cold bottles of water can cool your dog down on hot days. Don't put anything in a dog pack that can break. Dogs will bang the pack on rocks and trees when they wiggle through tight spots in the trail. Dogs also like to lie down in creeks and other wet spots so seal items in plastic bags. A good use for dog packs on day hikes around El Paso and Las Cruces is trail maintenance - your dog can pack out trash left by inconsiderate visitors before you.

🐾 Are dog booties a good idea?

Dog booties can be an asset, especially for the occasional canine hiker whose paw pads have not become toughened. Many trails in the desert, especially hillside routes, involve rocky terrain. In some places, broken glass abounds. Hiking boots for dogs are designed to prevent pads from cracking while trotting across rough surfaces. Used in winter, dog booties provide warmth and keep ice balls from forming between toe pads when hiking through snow.

"Dogs' lives are too short. Their only fault, really"
- Agnes Sligh Turnbull

The Desert Canine Hiking Kit

Even when taking short hikes it is a good idea to have some basics available for emergencies (as recommended by Dr. Mark Lennox, Crossroads Animal Clinic):

- Bandage material, vet wrap, cotton padding. If your dog burns or abrades his paws on hot or abrasive surfaces, you can pad his feet so he can walk.

- Antihistamine. If your dog is bitten by a snake or stung by a bee or wasp, give them antihistamine, about a milligram per pound.

- Cortisone tablets or aspirin as an anti-inflammatory. Dr. Lennox recommends that you talk to your veterinarian about which anti-inflammatory to take along for your dog.

- Needle nose pliers. Use these for plucking out stickers or cactus spines.

- Your veterinarian's phone number.

"If there are no dogs in Heaven,
then when I die I want to go where they went."
- Anonymous

Low Impact Hiking With Your Dog

Everytime you hike with your dog on the trail, you are an ambassador for all dog owners. Some people you meet won't believe in your right to take a dog on the trail. Be friendly to all and make the best impression you can by practicing low impact hiking with your dog:

- Pack out everything you pack in.

- Do not leave dog scat on the trail; if you haven't brought plastic bags for poop removal, bury it away from the trail and topical water sources.

- Hike only where dogs are allowed.

- Stay on the trail.

- Do not allow your dog to chase wildlife.

- Step off the trail and wait with your dog while horses and other hikers pass.

- Do not allow your dog to bark - people are enjoying the trail for serenity.

- Have as much fun on your hike as your dog does.

The Other End Of The Leash

Leash laws are like speed limits - everyone seems to have a private interpretation of their validity. Some dog owners never go outside with an unleashed dog; others treat the laws as suggestions or disregard them completely. It is not the purpose of this book to tell dog owners where to go to evade the leash laws or reveal the parks where rangers will look the other way at an unleashed dog. Nor is it the business of this book to preach vigilant adherence to the leash laws. Nothing written in a book is going to change people's behavior with regard to leash laws. So this will be the last time leash laws are mentioned, save occasionally when I point out the parks where dogs are welcomed off leash.

As a general rule, dogs should be kept on a leash in all city and state parks. (You will be fined if caught violating this rule.) On land managed by the Bureau of Land Management (clearly indicated in each hike), you may let dogs off the leash unless otherwise indicated at the hiking trail itself.

"And sometimes when you'd get up in the middle of the night you'd hear the reassuring thump, thump of her tail on the floor, letting you know that she was there and thinking of you."
                                                            - William Cole

Difficulty Rating

I have provided a "difficulty rating" of between "1" and "4" for each hike. A 1 indicates that the hike is easy to reach by highway or city roads and easy to traverse. A 2 indicates that the hike is easy to reach by highway or city roads but provides a more strenuous hike. A 3 indicates that the hike may be difficult to reach, using dirt or other un-graded roads, but the hike is easy or moderate and easily done in a day's trip. A 4 indicates that the hike may be difficult to reach and difficult to find and you should have an adventurous and intrepid spirit to attempt it.

An Important Website

The following link takes you to a website with links to various Department of the Interior Geological Survey quad maps of many of the hiking areas in this book. It is a great resource and if you plan to enjoy the hiking around El Paso and Las Cruces, you should learn how to read quad maps. You can view them for free at 125 dpi resolution, or you can order them at 250 dpi directly from the website:

http://www.topowest.com/main.html

How To Pet A Dog
Tickling tummies slowly and gently works wonders.
Never use a rubbing motion; this makes dogs
bad-tempered. A gentle tickle with the tips of the
fingers is all that is necessary to induce calm in a
dog. I hate strangers who go up to dogs with their
hands held to the dog's nose, usually palm towards
themselves. How does the dog know that the hand
doesn't hold something horrid? The palm should
always be shown to the dog and go straight down to
between the dog's front legs and tickle gently with a
soothing voice to acompany the action. Very often
the dog raises its back leg in a scratching movement,
it gets so much pleasure from this.
-Barbara Woodhouse

The Best of the Best...

The 10 Best Places To Hike With Your Dog
In the El Paso-Las Cruces Area

Blue Ribbon - Gila National Forest
America's first designated wilderness area features an incredible 3.3 million acres of unlimited canine hiking adventure. The variety of hikes include desert wilderness, forest lands, lakes, and aspen-covered peaks (reaching a height of 11,000 feet). The Mimbres Mogollon American Indians, who are known especially for their classic "black on white" pottery, left abundant evidence of their presence within the Gila, including spectacular cliff dwellings.

#2 - Lincoln National Forest
Your dog will find the home of Smokey the Bear much to her liking as well. There are more than one million acres in the Lincoln National Forest to explore, including desert canyons, cool pine forests and mountain peaks more than two miles high.

#3 - Rio Grande River
The levees running along the El Paso-Las Cruces section of the thousand-mile long international boundary that is the Rio Grande River are flat and wide and provide plenty of space for dogs to run around. This is easy canine hiking with plenty of opportunity to enjoy views of the mesa and surrounding mountain ranges.

#4 - Chihuahuan Desert Nature Park
Still a developing recreation area, the Chihuahuan Desert Nature Park offers an intriguing trail through the jagged Doña Ana Mountains but canine hikers can expand their day in this 960-acre park by heading for the hills as well.

#5 - Franklin Mountain State Park
With 24,000 acres of desert wilderness, Franklin Mountain is the largest state park entirely within city limits in the United States. Your dog can enjoy any length of romp through these billion year-old rocks.

#6 - White Sands National Monument

There are officially 6.2 miles of hiking trails in White Sands National Monument but just about any massive dune in the park's 200,000 acres is open to you and the dog.

#7 - Baylor Pass

This is a great moderate to strenuous hike, 6 miles one way through a canyon, peaking at around 6,430 feet. It provides great views of the Mesilla Valley to the west and the Tularosa Valley to the east. The trail is easy to follow and well-marked.

#8 - Irrigation Canals

Walking alongside irrigation waterways is generally easy because the paths are flat and well-maintained. There is no need to worry about dogs finding snakes, getting stickers in their paws, or finding a nose full of cactus spines. For people who struggle to find beauty in the harsh desert landscape, walking along canals or laterals provides something of a respite. You can wander through pecan orchards; globe willows, weeping willows, cottonwoods, and other trees grow along the paths, providing shade and green. Canals positioned in farmland criss-cross through chile, alfalfa and cotton fields.

#9 - Box Canyon & Picacho Peak

Picacho Peak is a dormant volcano, consisting of 959 acres of land, while Box Canyon is a great place to observe ancestral Rio Grande river deposits. During the Rio Grande's three million year history, it once traveled along a much wider alluvial plain than it does today. Box Canyon is also an excellent place to observe ancient volcanic rocks.

#10 - Aguirre Springs

A four-mile loop trail climbs to 6,500 feet through two life zones, the lower Sonoran and the the upper Sonaran. Every turn in the trail lends itself to a different perspective of outcroppings in the Organs such as the Needles, Rabbit Ears, and Baylor Peak; the Tularosa Valley; or White Sands Missile Range.

"A bone to the dog is not charity. Charity is the bone shared with the dog, when you are just as hungry as the dog."
- Jack London

14 Cool Things To See On El Paso-Las Cruces Hikes With Your Dog

"If your dog is fat," the old saying goes, "you aren't getting enough exercise." But walking the dog need not be just about a little exercise. Here are 14 cool things you can see in greater El Paso/Las Cruces while out walking the dog.

AIRPLANES.   Part of the hike through Box Canyon borders Las Cruces City Airport where you can observe vintage bi-planes and two-seaters droning past.

ARTWORK.   The lined paths and grassy areas of Chamizal National Memorial are a delight for dog walkers, as is *Our Heritage*, the mural painted on the outside wall of the Chamizal. It is a fine representative of Chicano/Hispanic art, and is one of the better preserved murals in the city. It depicts the historical blending of cultures along the United States and Mexico border.

BALD EAGLES.   Caballo Lake is a great spot to scan the skies for Bald and Golden eagles while your dog enjoys a rare desert doggie dip.

BEACH.   One of the most spectacular beaches in America is hundreds of miles from any ocean or lake. The white gypsum sand dunes at White Sands National Monument are the largest in the world. Visit at night in the summer when sand is cooler to the paw and the dunes are hauntingly beautiful.

DAMS.   The movement to build a dam on the Rio Grande started as early as 1896 but the plan was fraught with difficulty, not the least of which was the international implication of diverting water from Mexico. A water rights treaty was worked out on both sides of the border in 1906 and the Elephant Butte Dam, now a state park near Truth or Consequences, was completed a decade later. The concrete dam is one of the earliest and most important linchpins in the Bureau of Reclamation's overall plan for water in the West. Not as ornate, but a few years older, is the Leasburg Dam.

FORTS.   Camp Furlong, in the border town of Columbus, New Mexico, was the staging ground for General John "Black Jack" Pershing and his 10,000-man Punitive Expedition to hunt down Mexican revolutionary Pancho Villa in 1916. Pershing invaded 400 miles intoMexico but never caught Villa. Several buildings remain from Camp Furlong in Pancho Villa State Park: a rec hall, camp headquarters and the judge advocate's office among them.

FOSSILS.   The Robdelo Mountains contain an abundance of well-preserved vertebrate and invertebrate tracks from the Early Permian age 286 million years ago. Marine fossils are common on Crazy Cat Mountain trails.

GRAVES.   Concordia Cemetery contains 65,000 of them and you are welcome to tour this historic ground with your dog. The most famous gravesite, of Texas gunslinger John Wesley Hardin, wasn't even marked until 1965 - 70 years after his death.

HISTORIC BUILDINGS.   The entire town of Lincoln, New Mexico is listed on the National Register of Historic Places, a survivor of the bloody Lincoln County Wars. You and the dog can trace the events that turned an ordinary, unimpressive 17-year old William Bonney into the immortal "Billy the Kid."

OLD MINES.   The only tin mines on the North American continent can be found in Franklin Mountain State Park. You and the dog will stand and peer into these historic treasure troves. More dangerous are the abandoned mines on the east side of Bishop Cap.

RELIGIOUS ICONS.   Mt. Cristo Rey is the spot where two countries and three states come together and the summit is graced with the largest limestone cross in America, carved painstakingly for a year on the top of the mountain.

ROCKS.   Rockhound State Park encourages you to collect and keep samples of rock you discover on your canine hikes here. This includes an abundance of beautiful red Jasper, a form of fine-grained quartz. You may be lucky enough to find white Opal, Agate, quartz crystals or thunder-eggs, which may be cut open to reveal spectacular minerals and formations inside. There is a fifteen-pound limit for rock fishermen here.

TELESCOPES.   A hike to the top of Tortugas Mountain in Las Cruces will bring you and the dog to a 61-centimeter telescope reflector in use for the last 25 years, creating one of the largest planetary archives available in the U.S. It is currently being used to monitor storm systems on Jupiter.

VOLCANOES.   Hunts Hole and Kilbourne Hole are "maar volcanoes." They formed as a result of volcanic explosions, resulting from hot magma coming into contact with ground water or shallow surface water. This contact changed the surface water into steam, causing an explosion that blew volcanic glass and other material out of the ground. The black rock you see as you hike around the rim or descend into the crater is lava rock called Afton basalt.

"The best thing about a man is his dog."
- French Proverb

Cooper is ready to hike!

The 45 Best Places To Hike With Your Dog In The El Paso/Las Cruces Region

1
Gila National Forest

The Park

The Gila National Forest was America's first designated wilderness area and is today the sixth largest National Forest in the continental United States. It is an incredible 3.3 million acres of desert wilderness, forest lands, lakes, and aspen-covered peaks (reaching a height of 11,000 feet). The Mimbres Mogollon American Indians, known for their classic "black on white" pottery, left tangible evidence of their time within the Gila, including spectacular cliff dwellings built and lived in from the 1280s through the early 1300s. Archeologists speculate that Mogollon culture, which had thrived successfully in southern New Mexico since 200 A.D., collapsed from drought, warfare, disease, or some combination of factors - nobody knows for sure. After they disappeared, the Apache hunted and gathered here, including the famous Geronimo, who led his people to rebel against the reservation system. He was captured by United States Army regulars in 1886 in the bootheel of New Mexico.

several NM counties

Difficulty Rating
- From 1 to 4

Phone Number
- (505) 388-8201

Website
- fs.fed.us/r3/gila/

Admission Fee
- None

Directions
- From El Paso, take I-10 west through Las Cruces toward Deming. In Deming, take exit 82A and head north on US 180 towards Silver City. You can reach the Gila either by taking State Route 15 in Silver City or by taking State Route 152 in Santa Clara, shortly before Silver City, then turning right on State Route 35 toward Mimbres.

The Walks

In the Gila National Forest your dog will enjoy hundreds of hikeable miles in desert wilderness, through undisturbed canyons, along peaks and ridges, or besides streams and lakes. Hikes range from easy to strenuous in this mostly undeveloped land.

34

Dog Friendliness

Dogs are welcome on all trails here except the trail leading to the cliff dwellings, located at the Visitors' Center.

Traffic

Parts of the Gila National Forest are heavily used, but there are plenty of wilderness trails where you can seek solitude.

Canine Swimming

There are many lakes and rivers in the national forest to provide a stage for doggie aquatics. Beware of several hot springs - they are identified in the National Forest.

Trail Time

More than an hour.

"The greatest pleasure of a dog is that you may make a fool of yourself with him, and not only will he not scold you, but will make a fool of himself too."
- Samuel Butler

2

Lincoln National Forest

The Park

The Lincoln National Forest became famous around the world in May 1950 after an orphaned 5-pound bear cub was discovered clinging to a tree in a forest fire. The two-month old baby was enlisted as the living symbol for Smokey the Bear, a cartoon caricature created six years earlier to preserve forests for use in World War II. While Smokey lived in the National Zoo in Washington D.C., his symbolic persona grew to be the second most beloved character in the world, behind only Santa Claus. When Smokey died in 1976 he was returned to his home in Capitan and buried in a grave marked by a stone and plaque. Today, the Lincoln National Forest comprises over 1.1 million acres of mountain, sub-alpine forest and desert wilderness in three distinct tracts. Elevations rise to 11,500 feet.

In addition to hiking across the 1.1 million acres that make up Lincoln National Forest, you may consider hiking on the Mescalero Apache Indian Reservation. As you drive through the National Forest, you may drive on and off the reservation land.

The Mescalero Apaches are enterprising business owners, and offer skiing, hunting, and other recreational activities, which include hiking opportunities for you and your dog.

The Walks

A full day of canine hiking awaits in any of the three districts of the Lincoln National Forest. Many trailheads are easily located just off the main roads. Choose from easy rambles among the cool pines or strenuous climbs through the desert canyons.

Dog Friendliness

Dogs are permitted throughout the Lincoln National Forest.

Traffic

This is a popular hiking location; however, with a little searching, it is easy to find trails where few people travel.

Canine Swimming

There are streams and lakes throughout the Sacramento and Smokey Bear Districts for your dog to practice her dog-paddling.

Trail Time

More than an hour.

3

Rio Grande River

The Park

The Rio Grande, known on the Mexican side of the border as the Rio Bravo, begins life in the Colorado Rockies, snakes its way through New Mexico, and, just as it passes from New Mexico into Texas, transforms from functioning only as a river to become a thousand-mile international boundary between Mexico and the United States.

NM & TX counties
Difficulty Rating   - 1   Phone Number   - None   Website   - None   Admission Fee   - None   Directions   - See The Walks

In modern-day southern New Mexico and western-most Texas, not much is "grand" about the Rio Grande: it is barely a trickle weaving through a vast system of sand bars. During spring and summer, state officials working at the dam near Elephant Butte in New Mexico release more water; the sand bars disappear, the current picks up, and the Rio Grande begins to resemble a river.

Less than a hundred years ago, however, before the dam at Elephant Butte was constructed early in the 20th century, the Rio Grande flooded the El Paso valley regularly. For thousands of years the river was the region's major water source. Spanish conquistadors first crossed the Rio Grande near modern-day El Paso in 1535, then followed it north to the Pueblo Indian villages near Santa Fe and Taos. The Rio Grande soon became the guide for those following the Camino del Real (The Royal Road) from Mexico City up to Santa Fe. Today, almost five hundred years later, it still represents a major crossing point in the journey north.

The Walks

The Rio Grande abounds with great places to walk with your dog. Following are a few I recommend.

In Texas:

- Off Country Club Road. From I-10, take the Mesa Street exit. Going west, turn left onto Mesa; going east, turn right on Mesa. Continue on Mesa Street past Doniphan Road, where Mesa turns into Country Club Road. The river is about two miles from Doniphan. You can park on either side of the road and walk on the levee in either direction.

- Off Artcraft Road. From I-10, take the Artcraft exit. Follow the road west, until you reach the river.

- Near Canutillo. From I-10, take the Transmountain exit west to Doniphan Road. Turn right and take the first stoplight left. You will reach the river immediately.

- Near Vinton. From I-10, take the Vinton/Westway exit west (away from the River) and follow Vinton Road. The river is immediately past Doniphan.

In New Mexico:

- In Las Cruces, take I-10 west then turn off at Exit 139 as you head toward Deming, New Mexico. Turn right along S. Motel Blvd. Take a left when you reach Highway 70. The river is a short distance from the turnoff.

- Take Highway 478 from Anthony north towards Las Cruces. Great hiking spots occur in Anthony off Gadsden Road (which you can reach from Anthony's Main Street); on NM 226, which can be reached by a left turn off 478 in Berino; on NM 189, which can be reached by a left turn off 478 in Vado, New Mexico; and on NM 192, which can be reached by a left turn off of 478 in Mesquite, New Mexico.

- Take State Route 185 (N. Valley Road in downtown Las Cruces) from Las Cruces north to Hatch, New Mexico. This road crosses the river at several hiking locations.

The terrain is flat and wide, providing easy-walking. Levees running alongside both sides of the river provide plenty of space for dogs to run around. The walks feature views of the mesa and different mountain ranges, depending on where you hike: the Franklin Mountains, Mt. Cristo Rey, the Organ Mountains, the San Andres Mountains, or the Caballo Mountains. Given the number of songbirds in the area, the Rio Grande makes a great early morning walk. Keep an eye out for red-winged blackbirds in particular. Globe willows, salt cedars, and cottonwoods grow along the riverbanks and in people's backyards. The heavy, light green plants growing out of the tops of dying trees are mistletoe, a parasitic plant that kills its host.

Dog Friendliness

The levees of the Rio Grande are great places to take dogs! If you walk along the road or irrigation bank, rather than right alongside the river, be aware of the dogs and horses in back yards, or the cattle grazing along certain parts of the river who might get excited at the sight of your dog.

Traffic

Some of the hikes near the Rio Grande are popular for joggers, especially where the river runs through El Paso and Las Cruces. Between the two cities, however, you can expect to see few people. Keep an eye out for people riding bikes.

Canine Swimming

The Rio Grande gets more and more polluted the closer you get to Mexico.

Trail Time

More than an hour.

Cooper tests the Rio Grande and finds it dog-worthy.

4

Chihuahuan Desert Nature Park

The Park

In 1846, the U.S. military bloodlessly annexed this area as a territory of the United States. Lieutenant Colonel Cook, in command of the wagon train, crossed the Jornada del Muerto to Rincon, New Mexico, pioneering the first wagon road to the West Coast. Highway 70 follows part of this route. The 960-acre park was established in 1995 to further understanding of the Chihauhuan Desert, easternmost of the four great North American deserts. Still in development, future plans include a new road, a parking lot, restrooms, shade structures, interpretive signs for the hiking trail and an amphitheater.

Doña Ana County

Difficulty Rating
  - From 2
Phone Number
  - (505) 524-3334
Website
  - www.cdnp.org
Admission Fee
  - None
Directions
  - From Las Cruces, go 3 miles east of the I-25/Hwy 70 intersection on Hwy 70. Turn north at Jornada Road (a Shell station is on the corner). Travel approximately 6 miles north on Jornada Road, which becomes gravel. Turn left just before the cattle guard and the sign for the Jornada Experimental Range. Continue west along the fence line road for .9 miles to where the road becomes a Y. This is where the hiking trail begins. Desert has been cleared to serve as a parking lot.

The Walks

The Chihuahuan Desert Nature Park comprises part of the beautiful Doña Ana Mountains, with their jagged hills and peaks. One jagged hill as you drive towards the park on Jornada Road looks as if it has a backbone sticking out of the earth. Local Boy Scout Troop 179 has worked hard on developing a 1.5-mile hiking trail. The marked hiking trail is easy to follow, but you may also wish to venture into other parts of the mountains off the trail. Just mark your own trail and remember that the Organ and San Andres Mountains are east and so is your car. The trail offers breathtaking views of both mountain ranges, as well as the village of Organ and the valley between these eastern mountain ranges, as well as the village of Organ and the valley between these eastern mountains and the city of Las Cruces.

Dog Friendliness

Dogs are welcome throughout the park.

Traffic

You may occasionally encounter other people or school groups, but this park and these mountains allow a great deal of solitude.

Canine Swimming

None.

Trail Time

More than an hour.

*"They are superior to human beings as companions.
They do not quarrel or argue with you. They never talk about
themselves but listen to you while you talk about yourself,
and keep an appearance of being interested in the conversation."*
- Jerome K. Jerome

5

Franklin Mountain State Park

The Park

Franklin Mountains State Park, created in 1979, is the largest state park entirely within city limits in the United States. The park's boundaries enclose 24,000 acres of desert wilderness, including an entire mountain range in the Chihuahuan Desert. Approaching the park across Transmountain Road going east to west, you can easily identify the layered light green-to-white banded rocks of the Castner Formation to the north on the lower slopes of the mountain. These are the oldest rocks in the El Paso area, over a billion years old, formed under shallow seas that deposited layers of lime and clay. Volcanic activity interrupted this slow process. Driving through the mountain pass on Transmountain Road, you can observe Red Bluff granite, formed when magma cooled underground. Thunderbird Rhyolite, found in the red rock of the Thunderbird shape outlined on the west side of the Franklins, formed as a volcanic rock when some of the same magma erupted on the surface about 1 billion years ago. Around 500 million years ago, a shallow ocean flooded the area again. Marine sandstones, shales, and limestones accumulated until around 250 million years ago. These rock layers, which were deposited as flat beds, now tilt to the west. Rocks at the southern end of the mountains or within the main section of the park are the best places to study this.

City of El Paso

Difficulty Rating
  - 1-2
Phone Number
  - (915) 566-6441
Website
  - www.tpwd.state.tx.us/park/franklin/
Admission Fee
  - $3 per person
Directions
  - From I-10, take the Transmountain exit; head southeast towards the mountains. About 2 miles up the road, turn left into Franklin Mountain State Park.

The Walks

The park features many miles of hiking, either day hikes or backcountry hiking. Hikes range from strenuous to easy. Some of the trails (like West Cottonwood Springs) are steep, rocky, and difficult to maneuver if your dog is not well-behaved on the leash.

Dog Friendliness

Dogs are allowed only on leashes.

Traffic

This is a popular state park, so you will run into other hikers during your visit. Watch out for mountain bikers.

Canine Swimming

None.

Trail Time

More than an hour on most hikes.

6

White Sands National Monument

The Park

Covering almost 200,000 acres, White Sands National Monument is the world's largest area of gypsum sand dunes. It's a beautiful beach, minus the ocean. Its creation began about ten million years ago, as the center of a dome began to collapse, forming the Tularosa Basin and leaving the San Andres and Sacramento mountain ranges to the east and west. The mineral gypsum that forms the sand dunes is dissolved from the mountains during rainstorms. Normally, it would be carried off to the ocean by a river, but since this is an arid environment, it collects within the basin. The wind not only whittles gypsum crystals, but it transports them downwind, where they accumulate in sand dunes, creating ripples in the surface.

White Sands became a national monument in 1933. A local group, determined to promote Alamogordo, pushed for its development as a national park. Tom Charles, a leader in the group, suggested that its importance lay in the fact that everybody had "commercial" gypsum (the sort that makes casts, mortar, paint, or cement). But White Sands stood alone as being a form of "inspirational," or recreational, gypsum.

Otero County
Difficulty Rating - 1
Phone Number - (505) 679-2599
Website - www.nps.gov/whsa/
Admission Fee - $3 per person
Directions - From I-25 in Las Cruces, take I-70 east towards Alamogordo. White Sands will be on your left approximately 40 miles from Las Cruces. - From El Paso, take I-54 to Alamogordo. When you reach I-70, backtrack west (left) about 20 miles to White Sands.

The Walks

White Sands offers 6.2 miles of marked trails. But the entire park is great for kicking off your shoes and wandering around. It's easy

46

hiking, with miles of dunes. There is no need to blaze a trail or find one, although you should stick close to the road so you don't get lost since one sand dune looks just like another and there are no maps - the sand dunes are constantly shifting. Keep your eyes peeled for reptiles and rodents that have adapted to the white sands and are now a funny bleached white color.

During the summer, on the nights when the moon is full, the park stays open until midnight. The desert cools off at night, and the sands are beautiful by moonlight. It is worth the extra trip.

Dog Friendliness

Dogs are welcome throughout the park. On blazing summer days, the sand can be too hot for a dog's paws.

Traffic

Though many people visit White Sands, it is always possible to get off the trail and find a solitary dune.

Canine Swimming

None.

Trail Time

More than an hour.

7

Baylor Pass

The Park

For many years, this gap in the mountains was known as the Old Salt Trail Pass because settlers used it to haul salt from the salt flats at the base of the Guadalupe Mountains in West Texas. Eventually, it was named for John Robert Baylor (1822-1894), Confederate commander of the Second Texas Mounted Rifles, who patrolled the area between Ft. Bliss and Ft. Clark. Baylor reached Ft. Bliss in July 1861 and seized Mesilla, pursuing Union soldiers east into the Organ Mountains, where they surrendered at San Augustine Pass (Highway 70). Baylor exhibited strong antipathy towards American Indians, eventually raiding Chihuahua, where he boasted of killing Apaches. When he sent a letter to Captain Thomas Helm requesting the extermination of hostile Apaches, Confederate President Jefferson Davis removed him from command in 1862. Today Baylor Pass is managed by the Bureau of Land Management.

Doña Ana County

Difficulty Rating
- 2
Phone Number
- (505) 438-7542
Website
- www.nm.blm.gov/www/ new_home_2.html
Admission Fee
- None
Directions
- From El Paso, take I-10 west. In Las Cruces, take I-25 north, then turn onto I-70 east towards Alamogordo. Eleven miles later, turn right onto Baylor Canyon Rd. The parking lot for Baylor Pass Hiking Trail is 2 miles later.

The Walks

The trail though Baylor Pass is a great moderate to strenuous hike, 6 miles one way through a canyon, peaking at around 6,430 feet. You and your dog can enjoy superb views of the Mesilla Valley to the west and the Tularosa Valley to the east. The trail is easy to follow and well-marked.

Dog Friendliness

This is a great place to let your dog off the leash and explore the desert. Keep him close to the path and you will have little to worry about with regards to snakes or cactus.

Traffic

Only foot traffic and horseback riders are allowed; the Baylor Pass trail is generally lightly used.

Canine Swimming

None.

Trail Time

Over four hours to complete the out-and-back trail.

8

Irrigation Canals

The Park

American Indians started farming this land more than two thousand years ago, practicing irrigation in the Southwest for many hundreds of years before the Spanish arrived in 1535. Although this region has not always been as arid as it is now (over-grazing in the 19th century caused the process known as desertification), it has never had water resources like other parts of America. The transition from a hunting-gathering life to that of farming could only be accomplished by developing ways to move water from the rivers and the mountains to the lowlands, which had less water. Early settlers developed extensive systems of irrigation more than a thousand years ago, digging long winding ditches from rivers to their fields where they grew beans, corn, and squash. They stopped the flow of water by closing the ditch with dirt and sticks where it joined the river, then digging that out when they needed water.

When Spanish conquistadors arrived, they quickly saw the wisdom in the irrigation system; their tools allowed them to make better ditches faster, as well as better dams to stop the flow. They also instigated rules for sharing water, so that people got the water they needed. In the 19th century, English-speaking settlers to the Southwest had never used irrigation, but they quickly found how well it worked. The American Indian irrigation system, which was governed by Spanish water-rights laws, became American law.

several counties	
Difficulty Rating	- 1
Phone Number	- None
Website	- None
Admission Fee	- None
Directions	- See The Walks

The Walks

Irrigation waterways in the West are extensive, many of them with roads running along each side. Walking alongside them is generally easy because the paths are flat and well-maintained. There is no need to worry about dogs finding snakes, getting stickers in their paws, or finding a nose full of cactus spines. For people who struggle to find beauty in the harsh desert landscape, walking along canals or laterals provides something of a respite. You can wander through pecan orchards; globe willows, weeping willows, cottonwoods, and other trees grow along the paths, providing shade and green. Canals positioned in farmland criss-cross through chile, alfalfa and cotton fields.

A listing of each individual canal or lateral that provides great dog-walking would be so long, it would be silly. Simply drive through farm country and you'll spot potential ditches, canals, or laterals. Some canals are clearly on private land, while others skirt private land but are accessible publicly to pedestrians. Usually, it is obvious which are which. When in doubt, look for another lateral - you won't have far to go.

Here are a few roads where you will inevitably find hiking among irrigation canals, ditches, and laterals:

- Highway 28 or Highway 478 north, from El Paso to Las Cruces. You will pass several dozen potential walking spots along canals. You can also veer off Highway 28 onto any side road and you'll be sure to spot several great locations within seconds.

- Highway 185 north, from Las Cruces toward Hatch, New Mexico.

- Socorro Road, North Loop Drive, or Alameda Ave, east from the Avenue of the Americas in east El Paso.

- Country Club Road off Doniphan Road in El Paso, Texas, heading west.
- Old Mesilla, New Mexico - near Las Cruces, New Mexico. Park your car near the park in the middle of the town (which is east of the historic town plaza on Calle del Santiago.) Several laterals extend in different directions from the park, where they meet.

Dog Friendliness

These are perfect places to take dogs. Depending on whether the location of the canal is isolated or not, you may be able to let your dog off the leash. Just remember that many of these canals do pass along people's backyards, that they frequently cross streets, and that you may run into other people walking their dogs.

Traffic

Each canal, ditch, or lateral is different, but these are popular places where people walk their dogs, especially within city limits. If the canal meanders along fenced backyards in the city, you can depend on meeting people walking their dogs. If the canal is in the middle of farm country, you may not run into a single other dog.

Canine Swimming

When a canal is full, dogs could jump in for a swim, but I don't recommend it.

Trail Time

You can choose the duration of your hike along the canals.

As a young lawyer, 19th century Senator George Graham Vest of Missouri addressed the jury on behalf of his client, suing a neighbor who had killed his dog. Vest's speech has come to be known as "Tribute to the Dog."

The best friend a man has in the world may turn against him and become his enemy. His son or daughter that he has reared with loving care may prove ungrateful. Those who are nearest and dearest to us, those whom we trust with our happiness and our good name may become traitors to their faith. The money that a man has, he may lose. It flies away from him, perhaps when he needs it most. A man's reputation may be sacrificed in a moment of ill-considered action. The people who are prone to fall on their knees to do us honor when success is with us may be the first to throw the stone of malice when failure settles its cloud upon our heads.

The one absolutely unselfish friend that man can have in this selfish world, the one that never deserts him, the one that never proves ungrateful or treacherous is his dog. A man's dog stands by him in prosperity and in poverty, in health and in sickness. He will sleep on the cold ground, where the wintry winds blow and the snow drives fiercely, if only he may be near his master's side. He will kiss the hand that has no food to offer; he will lick the wounds and sores that come in an encounter with the roughness of the world. He guards the sleep of his pauper master as if he were a prince. When all other friends desert, he remains. When riches take wings, and reputation falls to pieces, he is as constant in his love as the sun in its journey through the heavens.

If fortune drives the master forth an outcast in the world, friendless and homeless, the faithful dog asks no higher privilege than that of accompanying him, to guard him against danger, to fight against his enemies. And when the last scene of all comes, and death takes his master in its embrace and his body is laid away in the cold ground, no matter if all other friends pursue their way, there by the graveside will the noble dog be found, his head between his paws, his eyes sad, but open in alert watchfulness, faithful and true even in death.

9

Box Canyon & Picacho Peak

The Park

Box Canyon and Spring Canyon have been managed by the Bureau of Land Management (BLM) for many years, but Picacho Peak was owned or leased privately until late 2000, when the Nature Conservancy bought it for $2.5 million, hoping they'd be able to work out a land swap with the BLM. The land swap went through in September 2002, and Picacho Peak has been added to the lands managed by the BLM.

Picacho Peak is a dormant volcano consisting of 959 acres. Box Canyon is a great place to observe ancestral volcanic rocks approximately 250 million years old, as well as ancestral river deposits, left here by the Rio Grande, which once traveled a much wider alluvial plain than it does today.

The Walks

You can take several roads and footpaths, depending on whether you want to hike the canyons located here or head up Picacho Peak. The washes, arroyos, and jeep paths are easy to find and follow; however, they are unmarked, so you should mark your own turn-offs to

Doña Ana County

Difficulty Rating
- 3
Phone Number
- (505) 438-7542
Website
- www.nm.blm.gov/www/ new_home_2.html
Admission Fee
- None
Directions
- Drive west on I-10 through Las Cruces to exit 135. The exit will curve around and head back towards the city on I-70. After you exit, make an immediate right turn across the median towards the airport (there will be a sign pointing the way, but no stop sign where you make the turn.) This is the I-10 frontage road. Drive 1.4 miles, then turn right (north) onto an unsigned graded dirt road. (NOTE: you will need to drive through a gate, with a sign requesting no stops for 2.2 miles. You are driving through private ranch land to reach the BLM managed land. Respect the sign and close the gate behind you after you drive through.) Drive 3.9 miles to a fork in the road. A BLM sign will indicate that this is Box Canyon Wildlife Habitat area. It is the starting point of the hike.

remember the direction of your car.

To reach Box Canyon, begin walking down the road toward the canyon for about .5 mile. Turn right off the road before you reach the dam and follow a dry wash down into Box Canyon. You'll reach the canyon below the dam, built by the Civilian Conservation Corps and near a large cottonwood tree. You can follow the arroyo downstream (heading east). In about half a mile, you can continue toward Box Canyon or turn left to hike up Spring Canyon. Continue as long as you desire past the intersecting road (which will lead you back to your car).

Dog Friendliness
Dogs are welcome on the trails here.

Traffic
The canyon is both dramatic and easily accessible and trails - although they will never be called crowded - receive more use than other BLM lands in the region.

Canine Swimming
None.

Trail Time
More than an hour.

10

Aguirre Springs

The Park

Like nearby Baylor Pass, the Pine Tree Trail at Aguirre Springs is part of the National Recreation Trail System. The Pine Tree Trail covers two life zones, beginning in the Lower Sonoran Life Zone (which rises from the valley floor up to about 5000 feet), where vegetation is dominated by creosote bush and mesquite plants. As the trail climbs to 6500 feet, it enters the Upper Sonoran Life Zone, where oak, juniper and piñon trees dominate. Creosote and yucca can't survive in these cooler elevations, although you may still find other desert plants typical of the Lower Sonoran Life Zone.

Doña Ana County

Difficulty Rating
- 2
Phone Number
- (505) 525-4300
Website
- None
Admission Fee
- $3 per vehicle. From May to September, the entrance gate opens at 8 a.m. and closes by 10 p.m. (except for campers). From October to April, the gate closes by 6 p.m., but you can still hike and picnic until 10 p.m.
Directions
- From Las Cruces I-25, take I-70 towards Alamogordo. After crossing San Augustin Pass, drive approximately three-quarters of a mile, watching for signs announcing Aguirre Springs to the right. Turn right and follow the road all the way to the fee area, approximately six miles.

The Walks

The Pine Tree Trail is a four-mile, easy-to-follow loop trail that can be completed in either direction. Breathtaking views haunt every turn on this easy to moderate hike with different perspectives of outcroppings in the Organs such as the Needles, Rabbit Ears, and Baylor Peak, or the Tularosa Valley. Unless the Organ Mountains have experienced a particularly dry year, you may see water when the trail crosses Anvil and Sotol Creeks. In the spring and late summer, this is a great place to look for wildflowers.

Bonus

Visible through most of the hike is the White Sands Missile Range where America's space age began with the firing of a Tiny Tim test booster at Launch Complex 33 on September 26, 1945. When testing missiles, it was important to retrieve small missile parts to analyze success or failure. These searches routinely wasted countless man-hours as ground recovery crews scoured vast expanses of desert for often-buried missile fragments. That all ended in 1961 with the introduction of the Missile Dogs: Dingo, a Weimaraner, and Count, a German Shorthair. For up to a year before firing, important components of a missile were sprayed with squalene, a shark-liver oil that the dogs could smell from hundreds of feet away. After a missile firing, the dog team was sent out for recovery as Dingo and Count sniffed out the scent object. With a 96% recovery rate, the program was so successful that other military and scientific agencies requested the services of the original Missile Dogs of White Sands.

Dog Friendliness

Dogs are requested to be on a leash at all times.

Traffic

There is no vehicular competition on Pine Tree Trail; it is hikers-only.

Canine Swimming

None.

Trail Time

More than an hour.

*"Dog. A kind of additional or subsidiary
Diety designed to catch the overflow and
surplus of the world's worship."*
                                        - Ambrose Bierce

11
Anthony's Gap

The Gap

The mountains here are flat sedimentary Paleozoic marine rocks, tilted steeply to the west. Erosion has created some of the apparent dips in the rock layers. This is a great place to observe the layers of sediment, and to notice how different vegetation grows along each layer. On the south side of Anthony's Gap, you may encounter some small quarries, especially of gypsum, a white, chalky mineral used to make casts and cement, among other things.

The Walks

There are several jeep roads, trails, and washes that are easy to follow to the east or to the west, to the north or the south, providing miles of great hiking in the foothills or climbing the peaks. North Anthony's Nose, to the north of Anthony's Gap, peaks at 5,388 feet. Watch for the agave, a small cactus plant that grows close to the ground in a bundle of small green spear-like leaves. It grows in abundance here and stings if you (or your dog) get stuck!

Doña Ana County

Difficulty Rating
- 2
Phone Number
- (505) 438-7542
Website
- www.nm.blm.gov/www/ new_home_2.html
Admission Fee
- None
Directions
- Anthony's Gap is Highway 404, located off I-10 near Anthony, New Mexico, at exit 162. To reach the north end of the Franklins (and Anthony's Nose), take any number of roads that lead off to the right of 404. Drive toward the hills and mountain ranges located southeast until you reach a spot where you want to hike. To reach North Anthony's Nose, drive 4.3 miles east until you see large white gas pipes protruding from the ground on the north (left) side of the highway. Turn left onto the unmarked road and proceed through the gate. (It will be closed and hooked up, with a sign that says, "Natural Gas Company," but it is BLM land and you have right of public access. Drive on through.) Park just beyond the exposed pipes near a second fence with an opening leading toward the mountains.

Dog Friendliness

Dogs can roam free here.

Traffic

There is little competition for the trails in Anthony's Gap.

Canine Swimming

None.

Trail Time

More than an hour.

Cooper takes advantage of the shade of a mesquite tree.

59

12
Bishop Cap

The Mountain

Bishop Cap is a remarkable mountain, almost trianglular in shape and highly visible from the freeway, rising to a peak of 5,419 feet from a base of around 4,500 feet. Nestled in the midst of hundreds of acres of BLM managed land, it is composed of layers of sedimentary rock, which form when sand, silt, or clay are deposited in layers or beds, then undergo either compaction or cementation, hardening to become rock. Bishop Cap is made up of many such layers, deposited between 245-550 million years ago. The rocks visibly tilt to the west toward the river as a result of fault activity and block rotation, all part of the Rio Grande Rift activity.

Doña Ana County

Difficulty Rating
 - 2-3
Phone Number
 - (505) 438-7542
Website
 - www.nm.blm.gov/www/ new_home_2.html
Admission Fee
 - None
Directions
 - From El Paso, drive west on I-10 to exit 155 (Vado). Turn right and follow the road east approximately 2 miles until you reach the first set of power lines. Park here and begin hiking along the road.

The Walks

Your hike begins along the road tracing the power lines, but you can branch off whenever you want, heading northeast toward Bishop Cap. Possible branchoff points include Vado Arroyo, which snakes around the mountain along the eastern side. If you choose this option, you will eventually need to leave the arroyo and head out across open mesa. Another possible stepping off point is a dirt road leading north or northeast toward Bishop Cap. Despite the fact that there isn't a marked trail (although roads do lead up the mountain), the hike is easy to follow because there are several landmarks. Keep in mind that your car is parked south and southwest, along the first set of power lines, and that Bishop Cap, which is a well marked landmark, is north and east of

Bishop Cap, which is a highly visible landmark, is north and east of your car.

Dog Friendliness

Great! Let your dog free to roam. There is less wildlife to worry about here than in some other areas like the West Mesa. But still be careful of the mines on the east side of the hill.

Traffic

You will run into very few people in this desert wilderness hike.

Canine Swimming

None.

Trail Time

More than an hour.

13

McKelligan Canyon Park

The Park

McKelligan Canyon is a large canyon on the northeast side of the Franklin Mountains, ostensibly part of the state park, but very different in its trails and its views of Ft. Bliss and the vast plains of west Texas. For many years, McKelligan Canyon was avoided after night, not just because of bobcats but also because of vandals. Once trashy and plagued by graffiti artists, McKelligan Canyon has been included as part of a concerted community effort to make the mountains safe and clean for families and hikers.

City of El Paso

Difficulty Rating
 - 2
Phone Number
 - (915) 566-6441
Website
 - None
Admission Fee
 - None
Directions
 - From I-10, take I-54 heading towards Alamogordo. Take the Fred Wilson Ave. Exit and turn left onto Fred Wilson. Follow the road west until you reach Alabama. Take a left on Alabama. A short distance later, turn right onto McKelligan Canyon Road.

The Walks

McKelligan Canyon offers multiple options for hiking as soon as you turn off Alabama onto McKelligan Canyon Road - trails lead into the mountain. Notice how the range is separated into two blocks; the fault line runs down the middle of the canyon and dips to the east. A couple of easily visible rocks that you may be able to identify are the Red Bluff Granite (magma which cooled below the surface of the earth over 550 million years ago), and the Bliss Formation (red-brown beds of sedimentary rock deposited near the shore of a tropical sea between 500-550 million years ago).

You can also drive to the end of the road, beyond the amphitheatre, and park at a picnic site. From there, you have a choice of six or seven small hills and peaks to climb. Watch for the Great Horned Owl, a large bird with a wingspan of four and a half feet;

the Greater Roadrunner, a swift runner that rarely flies, sticking to the foothills and lower slopes; the Red-tailed Hawk, which has a white stripe on its wings; and the Golden Eagle, which looks silver underneath.

Hikes range from moderate to strenuous. Some paths are rocky and steep, while others are dirt and smooth. This is true desert hiking. Bring a hat and lots of water; don't expect to see trees.

Dog Friendliness

Like the rest of the Franklin Mountains, dogs are perfectly welcome here. But also like the rest of the Franklin Mountains, the paths can be steep and a little slippery with rocks, so be careful.

Traffic

McKelligan Canyon is a popular picnic park but don't expect competition on these desert trails.

Canine Swimming

None.

Trail Time

More than an hour.

"Money will buy a pretty good dog
but it won't buy the wag of his tail."
- Josh Billings

14

The Robledo Mountains

The Mountains

The Robledo Mountains consist of 12,946 acres of desert wilderness and ranch land. The high mesas found in the Robledos, as in the Sierra de las Uvas, preserve the kind of grasslands that covered this region more than 200 years ago. The Robledos feature some unusual desert attractions, including yucca stalks that grow as high as trees and the kind of isolation that means you're more likely to spot oryx or mule deer. You will encounter limestone, dolomite, and whitish rhyolite in the Robledos.

The Walks

Hikes in the Robledos can range from moderate to strenuous, depending on how high you climb. Jeep roads and arroyos are the main markers of the trails on this mountain; these well-marked trails all lead to various destinations in the Robledos, sometimes criss-crossing each other. It is certainly possible to stray off the beaten path, but only do so if you don't get lost easily. Mark the roads you take if you make a lot of turns. This is a great place to take your dog if you crave solitude and peace.

Doña Ana County

Difficulty Rating
- 3
Phone Number
- (505) 438-7542
Website
- www.nm.blm.gov/www/ new_home_2.html
Admission Fee
- None
Directions
- From Las Cruces, drive north on I-25. Take exit 9 (Doña Ana) and turn left to go under the overpass. Drive for two miles on New Mexico Highway 320, driving over the railroad tracks. Turn right on New Mexico Highway 185 and then approximately half a mile later, turn left onto Shalem Colony Trail. Shortly after crossing the Rio Grande, turn right onto Rocky Acres Trail (County Road DO-13). Veer left at the Y-intersection a short while later, a dirt road that proceeds directly into the mountains. Follow it approximately .5 mile, then park on the left.

Dog Friendliness

You can let your dog roam free here, but keep an eye on the ground for rattlesnakes.

Traffic

None. It is rare to encounter anyone in the Robdelos, no matter how many days you spend there. In fact, make sure someone knows where you are going and when you plan to be back.

Canine Swimming

None.

Trail Time

More than an hour.

"Any man who does not like dogs and want them does not deserve to be in the White House."
— Calvin Coolidge

15

Sierra de las Uvas

The Park

The Sierra de Las Uvas consist of 7,283 acres of desert wilderness and ranch land. The mountains are a block of earth that tilts to the west. Deep canyons create a number of high mesas which, to the east, become foothills and drainages that lead eventually to the Robledo Mountains.

The Walks

The jeep roads are easy to follow, as are the ditches and washes that you will encounter. Hikes can be highly variable, depending on which bend in the road or which wash, arroyo, or hill you find most intriguing. The variety and variability of hikes is great here - plant life appears to have access to a much better water source than surrounding desert areas. The prickly pear cactus, for instance, looks greener and healthier in the Sierra de las Uvas than on other hikes indicated in this book. Prickly pear is a fast-growing species of cacti that can grow over 6 feet tall, with pads over eight inches in diameter.

Doña Ana County

Difficulty Rating
  - 3
Phone Number
  - (505) 438-7542
Website
  - www.nm.blm.gov/www/
    new_home_2.html
Admission Fee
  - None
Directions
  - Follow I-10 west out of Las Cruces, towards Deming. Exit at #127, and make a right turn onto the frontage road. About half a mile later, turn left onto Corralitos Road, which is also County Road 9A. Follow this road 10.6 miles. You'll pass the ranch and the road will curve left and pass between the Sleeping Lady Hills (to your left) and the Rough and Ready Hills (to your right). At this point, you'll reach a fork in the road. Any spot up to the fork in the road has the potential for leading to a good hiking spot, but to get to the Sierra de las Uvas, bear right at the fork and continue along the road for another 12 miles. A great place to start your exploration of the Sierra de las Uvas begins here, 22.6 miles from the frontage road. The paved road continues up the mountain, but a gate prevents the general public from continuing up the road via car. Straight north, an unimproved dirt road is your entrance to the Sierra de las Uvas.

Native Americans used both the green pads and the red fruit as an important food source. (You can buy cactus jam, "nopalitos," and other food items derived from the prickly pear in grocery stories and tourist shops in the region.)

A few creepy-crawly creatures to watch for: The Horny Toad, also known as the Texas Horned Lizard, primarily eats ants. When startled, horny toads shoot a small stream of blood from pores that are located near the eyes. The Common Collared Lizard is the only iguana species in the Chihuahua Desert. It has a black and white collar across the back of its neck and green sides. Females may have reddish-orange marks on the neck and side. They raise their tails and run on their hind legs, resembling a little dinosaur. Harvester Ants are worth watching, as well. They can grow up to a half inch in length. Their anthills are easy to spot: usually a large pile of sand or gravel surrounds the hole. They are very active during the day, carrying food on their backs to their nests. On occasion, ants carry a startling amount of weight on their backs, such as a small baby lizard.

Dog Friendliness

This is a great place for dogs! Let them run free. If you have a dog that likes to herd cows, however, you might consider putting her on a leash.

Traffic

This is true solitude and desert wilderness hiking. Take a compass, plenty of water and a cell phone along if you have one.

Canine Swimming

None.

Trail Time

More than an hour.

16

Caballo Lake State Park

The Park

Caballo Lake was built in the 1930s as part of an ongoing attempt to control water flow that had begun two decades earlier with the construction of the Elephant Butte reservoir eleven miles to the north. This prevented flooding as far south as El Paso, Texas and allowed farmers to irrigate their lands during the growing seasons through an elaborate system of canals that stretched for hundreds of miles.

Truth or Consequences, the city located just north of Caballo and south of Elephant Butte, was known as Palomas Hot Springs until 1950. It changed its name to the popular radio program "Truth or Consequences" in exchange for a live coast-to-coast program. With the name change, state senator Burton Roach argued, Truth or Consequences's mineral baths would be advertised for free every Saturday night, every time the radio program aired.

Sierra County
Difficulty Rating - 1
Phone Number - (505) 743-3942
Website - www.emnrd.state.nm.us/ nmparks/PAGES/PARKS/ CABALLO/CABALLO.HTM
Admission Fee - $4 per vehicle
Directions - From El Paso, take I-10 east towards Las Cruces. In Las Cruces, take the I-25 juncture north for 59 miles. Turn off at exit 59 and turn right at the end of the ramp onto U.S. 187. To reach Caballo Lake State Park, continue straight for .8 of a mile and turn right. Proceed to the pay station.

The Walks

Caballo State Park consists of 11,000 acres of reservoir and beach. It is fifteen miles long, with over 50 miles of shoreline. You can walk along the dam near the river section of the park, and hike up the primitive road beyond the dam; you can also hike along the river and lakeside and in the park itself if it's not too crowded. Along the lake, the shore can be pebbly in spots, which doesn't encourage walking. However, the hiking and walking within Caballo State Park is not the high point of the visit. The lake is great swimming for both dogs and humans, and the river is also a great place for dogs to go swimming. In fact, this is one of very few swimming spots in southern New Mexico or west Texas, so if your dog loves to swim, take advantage of it.

Dog Friendliness

Dogs are perfectly welcome, although they should be on a leash if they are not in the water.

Traffic

During the summer, expect a lot of people to be fishing, boating and picnicking, especially on weekends.

Canine Swimming

Yes, yes and yes.

Trail Time

Less than an hour.

Can this really be a lake in my desert?

17

Elephant Butte State Park

The Park

The movement to dam the Rio Grande in this area started as early as 1896. Construction started in November of that year, but landowners downstream in El Paso and Mexico howled that they would lose water to farmers who irrigated upstream. The Supreme Court became involved in the legal battle and put a stop to construction, arguing that the Rio Grande was a navigable stream, and thus could not be blocked. Eventually, the Federal Government blocked private enterprise, created an agreement for water delivery with Mexico, and started construction on the dam in 1911. The dam was completed on May 13, 1916. The State Park was completed in 1965 and has been one of New Mexico's most popular state parks ever since.

Sierra County

Difficulty Rating
- 1
Phone Number
- (505) 744-5421
Website
- www.emnrd.state.nm.us/
  nmparks/PAGES/PARKS/BUTTE/
  BUTTE.HTM
Admission Fee
- $4 per vehicle
Directions
- From Las Cruces, drive on I-25 north to Exit 83. Follow signs directing you to the park's entrance.

The Walks

The 36,000 acre park has two improved trails, as well as over 200 miles of shoreline, much of which is great for walking and swimming, although you can't always walk precisely along the shoreline because of bushes or campers. The park has plans for developing more trails.

Dog Friendliness

Dogs are welcome, though they should be leashed. The shoreline can be pebbly in places, which can be hard on paws, but the water and sandy shores conspire to create a canine playground.

Traffic

Elephant Butte is a popular spring and summertime location. On weekends and holidays, it can be crowded. New Mexico's moderate winter temperatures, however, makes this park a great place to visit in fall or winter when the crowds lessen.

Canine Swimming

Absolutely. Like Caballo Lake, Elephant Butte is an excellent place for canine and human aquatics.

Trail Time

More than an hour.

"A dog teaches a boy fidelity, perserverance, and to turn around three times before lying down."

- Robert Benchley

18
City of Rocks
State Park

The Park

City of Rocks is almost 35 million years old, formed when a volcano erupted in an explosion 1,000 times hotter and greater than the eruption of Mount St. Helens in 1980. As the volcanic layer cooled, it cracked and splintered. Rain, snow, and wind further eroded the rocks into unusual shapes. Park rocks consist of tuff, volcanic rock made up of pyroclastic material - fragments of rock, mineral, and volcanic glass. This particular volcanic tuff is known as Kneeling Nun tuff because a rock formation to the north looks like a kneeling nun.

Grant County

Difficulty Rating
- 1
Phone Number
- (505) 536-2800
Website
- www.emnrd.state.nm.us/
nmparks/PAGES/PARKS/
CITYROCK/CITYROCK.HTM
Admission Fee
- Take I-10 West toward Deming. and take exit 82A, heading north on U.S. 180 towards Silver City. Follow signs to City of Rocks State Park, turning north (right) on Route 61. After 4.7 miles, turn left off 61 onto a side road that leads to City of Rocks.

City of Rocks has long been a camping and recreational destination. The Mimbres Indians settled in the area about 750-1250 A.D., leaving traces of their presence in arrowheads and pottery shards. (They are famous for their classic "black on white" pottery.) Apache Indians next moved into the area, and then Spanish explorers, following the Rio Grande in search of gold, arrived in the late 1500s. Captain Cooke passed south of here, and the Butterfield Overland Mail Route, which transported mail from St. Louis to San Francisco (a trip that took 23 days and 23 hours to complete), passed near here during its three years in operation (1858-1861). American settlers followed the railroad and camped and picnicked here, but the area did not become an official New Mexico state park until 1952.

The Walks

City of Rocks provides a fairyland for rock enthusiasts. A maintained trail travels through the rock formations from one end of the park to the other, but you can wander at will through the rocks. Though some rocks may be too steep for dogs to climb, they are easy to maneuver through, and for dogs who like to explore, each turn provides another adventure.

Dog Friendliness

Dogs are welcome, but they must be on a leash. Except for climbing on the rock formations themselves, the ground is easy on a dog's paws. Rangers occasionally spot a coyote, but as long as you stick to the area designated as a state park, your dog need not worry about confronting one.

Traffic

During the spring and summer, many people camp here. It is a popular state park. You shouldn't be overwhelmed by people, however because it is a large state park.

Canine Swimming

None.

Trail Time

More than an hour.

19

Leasburg Dam State Park

The Park

Leasburg Dam State Park is situated on part of the land that belonged to Ft. Selden, established in 1865 to protect the settlements of the Mesilla Valley from the Gila Apaches. The post was abandoned in 1891. The dam, built in 1908, is one of the oldest dams in the state.

The Walks

Though Leasburg consists of 140 acres of park, much of that space is reserved for parking. The path is easy and short, trailing through flat desert mesa and alongside the river. The dominant vegetation here, like all that in the Chihuahuan Desert, is creosote bush, prickly pear, and some mesquite. However, desert willows salt cedar and tamarisk grow close to the river.

Sierra County

Difficulty Rating
- 1
Phone Number
- (505) 524-4068
Website
- www.emnrd.state.nm.us/ nmparks/PAGES/PARKS/ LEASBURG/LEASBURG.HTM
Admission Fee
- $4 per vehicle
Directions
- Take I-10 towards Las Cruces, then I-25 north to Albuquerque. Take exit 19 and turn left at the stop sign at the end of the ramp. For desert hiking, turn right onto Richard Cooper Memorial Drive approximately a mile later. For walking near the river and for swimming, continue driving past Richard Cooper Memorial Drive 1.3 miles, then turn right onto Leasburg Dam Road and follow until you reach the Ranger Station.

You and your dog can also follow the park's roads, and head down to the river for a swim. The park provides great views of the Rio Grande and Leasburg Dam, the Robledo Mountains to the south, the Sierra de las Uvas to the West, and Doña Ana Peak to the east. Part of the road follows the railroad, which is something to watch out for. Trains do pass by a few times during the day and evening.

Dog Friendliness

Dogs are welcome in the park and free "mutt mitts" - biodegradable pick-up mitts - are located near the comfort station. Rangers emphasize to travelers that pets can not be left in the car or outside in the sun - they must be in the shade, and left with water and food.

Traffic

During the summer, expect to meet people spending the day with their families, picnicking and barbecuing. It's not crowded, but it is hard to get away from people.

Canine Swimming

Leasburg Dam State Park is a prime destination for dogs looking to work on their dog-paddling.

Trail Time

Less than an hour.

*"My dog can bark like a Congressman,
fetch like an aide, beg like a press secretary
and play dead like a receptionist."*
- Gerald Solomon

20

Kilbourne Hole &
Hunts Hole

The Holes

Hunts Hole and Kilbourne Hole are "maar volcanoes." They formed when hot magma from the earth's mantle came into contact with ground water or shallow surface water. This contact changed the surface water into steam, causing an explosion that blew volcanic glass and other material out of the ground. The black rock you see is lava rock called Afton basalt. It is possible to find chunks ("bombs") of black volcanic material that include a light green glassy-looking crystalline mineral called olivine. On the east ridges, dune material has piled up from westerly winds. The West Mesa, including Kilbourne Hole and Hunts Hole, is managed by the Bureau of Land Management.

The Walks

Walking around the rim or descending into the craters provides miles of good canine hiking, although on the east slopes of both craters, loose dune material can make footing treacherous at times. The

Doña Ana County

Difficulty Rating
 - 3
Phone Number
 - (505) 438-7542
Website
 - www.nm.blm.gov/www/
 new_home_2.html
Admission Fee
 - None
Directions
 - From I-10, turn off on the Vinton/Westway exit (exit #2). Going west, turn left onto Vinton Road. Going east, turn right onto Vinton Road. Follow it 1.8 miles, across Doniphan Road and the Rio Grande. At the Y, turn left onto North Vinton Road and follow it 2 miles to State Highway 28, and make another left. Make an immediate right onto Mercantil Road (State Highway 182 West). The road forks less than a mile ahead. Take the right fork for 1/10 of a mile to Alvarez Road, and turn right. Alvarez Road turns into a dirt road; take the left road at the next fork which becomes County Rd. A-20. Follow it 6.7 miles, past the railroad tracks, to a "T" in the road, and turn right. About 4/10 of a mile later, turn left onto County Road A-14. Follow this road 12 miles until you see a side road to your right. Turn onto it and you'll come to the rim of Hunts Hole. Farther down this road, heading north to northwest, you'll reach Kilbourne Hole.

hikes provide great views of the Juárez Mountains to the south, the Franklin Mountains to the east, the Organ Mountains to the northeast, and a close up of the East Portrillo Mountains to the southwest and Mt. Riley to the west. Keep an eye out for nighthawks, rabbits, and lizards. In May, the chollas bloom with brilliant magenta colors and the yucca bloom with bridal-like ivory-colored bouquets.

Dog Friendliness

Land managed by the BLM is frequently isolated, set aside and rented out as ranch land. As such, it's a great place to let your dog run free. This is wild desert, though, so watch for snakes and coyotes.

Canine Swimming

None.

Traffic

Expect a solitary visit. Bring a reliable car or a cell phone to the West Mesa. It is a long way to walk if your car breaks down.

Trail Time

More than an hour.

21
Crazy Cat Mountain

The Trail

The trail on this part of the Franklin Mountains - which is not part of the state park - traverses sedimentary rock layers known as the underlying El Paso Formation and the overlying Montoya Formation. Sedimentary rocks are layers of sand or clay that are deposited in beds, and eventually undergo processes that harden them into rock. The El Paso Formation is older than the Montoya, but both were deposited between 440-500 million years ago. The El Paso Formation was deposited as limestone in a shallow tropical ocean. Eventually, as the seas receded, they began to undergo erosion. When the sea level rose again, the Montoya Formation was deposited. A fault line runs directly under Crazy Cat Mountain and Rim Road, making a beeline through downtown El Paso.

El Paso County

Difficulty Rating
- 2
Phone Number
- None
Website
- crl.nmsu.edu/~mleisher/bmba/
MonksArroyoPark.jpg *(trail maps)*
Admission Fee
- None
Directions
- From I-10, take the Schuster/UTEP exit. Head up Schuster toward Mesa Street. Turn left on Mesa. Make an immediate right onto Rim Road. Follow Rim Road until it forms a Y with Scenic Drive. Follow the road left (away from Scenic Drive). As the road curves around, before it starts heading south again, park your car where a dirt road begins curving up the mountain. This is the starting point of the hike.

The Walks

Criss-crossing paths and roads are easy to make out on Crazy Cat Mountain; they are well-maintained by the hikers and mountain-bikers who frequent them. The hike is moderate to strenuous in nature, and the paths tend to go up and down hills, sometimes steeply. This is a paw-friendly route - no need to worry about stray rocks, stones, or thorns that might make walking difficult.

Dog Friendliness

You can let your dog off the leash to trot the trails here.

Traffic

Crazy Cat Mountain is a popular spot for walking dogs and for mountain biking in the El Paso City area.

Canine Swimming

None.

Trail Time

More than an hour.

*"We are alone, absolutely alone on this chance
planet; and, amid all the forms of life that
surround us, not one, excepting the dog,
has made an alliance with us."*

- Maurice Maeterlinck

22

Rockhound State Park

The Park

For many years, Apache Indians hunted and made camp in this area. The Buffalo Soldiers, a regiment of African-American soldiers, covered the entire Southwest and were particularly prominent here, protecting settlers from Indian raids. Their name is one of honor, given by American Indians because of their fighting spirit, which was brave and courageous like the buffalo's. Rockhound State Park, set on the western slope of the Little Florida Mountains, was established in 1966. It was named for its most obvious feature: its abundance of pretty rocks. The Florida Mountains themselves were named by Spanish explorers for the wildflowers and cactus that bloom in the spring (a feature that makes it a popular location to visit in April and May, or anytime after a good rain).

Luna County

Difficulty Rating
 - 2
Phone Number
 - (505) 546-6182
Website
 - www.emnrd.state.nm.us/
 nmparks/PAGES/PARKS/
 ROCKH/ROCKH.HTM
Admission Fee
 - $4 per vehicle
Directions
 - Take I-10 west toward Deming. In Deming, turn off the highway at exit 82. Turn south (left) on NM 11 and drive 5 miles, then turn left (east) on NM 141. The road will make a T with 143. Continue right on 143 and stay on the road until you reach the State Park. The park is located about 9 miles after you turn on NM 141.

The Walks

The Park Trail is short and moderate, easy to follow, with superb views and a good opportunity to observe desert plant life. Take care at the beginning of the hike - the rocks used to line the path can be tough on tender paws. The adjacent state and federal land extending east and north of the trail provides great places to wander with your dog. Wildlife includes the ubiquitous rattlesnake, coyote, and wild dog. In 1976, local ranchers introduced the Persian ibex mountain goat, and on rare days, you may glimpse one or two on the hillsides.

Dog Friendliness
Dogs should be kept on leashes although encounters with wild animals in Rockhound State Park are rare.

Traffic
Somewhat off the beaten track, there is little competition on the partk trail.

Canine Swimming
None.

Trail Time
Less than an hour.

"Properly trained, a man can be dog's best friend."
- Corey Ford

23

Spring Canyon State Park

The Park

Spring Canyon is an addendum to Rockhound State Park, although it is set in a different area of the Florida Mountains. The interior is reached only on foot or by horse. The Floridas were once covered by an ancient sea, emerging as an island about 300 million years ago. If you look carefully, you can spot some of the same fossils that you can see in the Franklin Mountains near El Paso.

For many years, the government mined fluorspar and manganese here. Manganese hardens steel and is used to manufacture flashlight batteries. These mining operations continued through World War II and the 1950s.

Luna County

Difficulty Rating
 - 2-3
Phone Number
 - (505) 546-6182
Website
 - www.emnrd.state.nm.us/
 nmparks/PAGES/PARKS/
 ROCKH/ROCKH.HTM
Admission Fee
 - $4 per vehicle
Directions
 - Take I-10 west toward Deming. In Deming, turn off the highway at exit 82. Turn south (left) on NM 11 and drive 5 miles, then turn left (east) on NM 141. The road will make a T with 143. Continue right on 143 then veer to the right on to 198 and follow the road approximately 3 miles to the entrance of the State Park. (There are signs pointing the way.)

The Walks

As a day use area, Spring Canyon offers miles and miles of undeveloped, rugged trails. Be prepared for the wilds if you go hiking here - take plenty of water for yourself and your dog, and wear good shoes and a hat as protection from the sun. With its unrelenting summer heat, Spring Canyon is a place better left for cooler weather canine hiking.

Dog Friendliness

This wilderness area is a great place to go for solitude and to let your dog off the leash. You should watch out for rough terrain and stickers that may be hard on your dog's paws. As well, you should watch out for wildlife (rattlesnakes and coyotes).

Traffic

It is almost an event of cosmic intervention to encounter a horse, mountain biker or fellow hiker on the trail during an outing at lightly used Spring Canyon State Park.

Canine Swimming

None.

Trail Time

More than an hour.

"No animal should ever jump up on the dining room furniture unless...he can hold his own in the conversation."

- Fran Liebowitz

24
Rio Bosque

The Park

The University of Texas at El Paso's Center for Environmental Resource Management (CERM) is attempting to recreate the mix of habitats historically found at the Rio Grande in pre-settlement conditions in this 375 acres of desert wetlands. For thousands of years, the Rio Grande flowed freely through the region, flooding the plains and creating swampy areas where wildlife and plant life flourished. Since 1996, the Boy Scouts, students, government agents, and other volunteers have worked to restore the wetland and riparian habitats to these water-controlled lands. Still in its nascent stage, plans are in place at the Rio Bosque Wetlands to develop a Visitor Station, interpretive displays, and the Discovery Pond - a permanent pond where visitors can study up close the organisms that live in water.

City of Socorro

Difficulty Rating
- 1
Phone Number
- (915) 747-5494
Website
- www.cerm.utep.edu/riobosque
Admission Fee
- None
Directions
- Take I-10 East to Avenue of the Americas. Head southwest towards the Zaragosa Bridge. Get off at Pan American Drive, and turn left. Drive 1.5 miles, which will get you to a bridge crossing the canal. Cross the bridge and turn left, heading down the dirt road alongside the canal. You will reach the first entrance approximately .5 miles later; 1 mile will bring you to a second entrance and a parking area; 1.6 miles will bring you to the beginning of the developed hike and another parking area.

The Walks

The restored desert wetlands include three marked trails, only one that is fully realized as of this writing and is your best way to experience the park. Keep in mind that while CERM works to return this area to its natural habitat, weeds and paw-puncturing stickers and glass abound. Stick to the trails or roads.

Dog Friendliness

Dogs are welcome in the Rio Bosque Wetlands although as the park becomes more developed, there may be more regulations.

Traffic

Still relatively unknown, you are most likely to encounter other people only if you go during the twice-monthly walking tours or on a Saturday when the park hosts a community workday.

Canine Swimming

None.

Trail Time

Less than an hour.

25

New Mexico State University

The Campus

New Mexico State University started in 1888 as the New Mexico College of Agriculture and Mechanic Arts, prior to New Mexico becoming a state. The school changed its name to New Mexico State University in 1960, but it is still known as an agricultural school. The 900-acre campus includes long sloping lawns and is swathed in tall pine trees. The International Mall traverses the length of the campus, with many side trails and roads curving off to the left and right. The east side of the campus has a hilly expanse of grass, while the west side, called the Horseshoe, has a park set down between two roads.

City of Las Cruces

Difficulty Rating
- 1
Phone Number
- (505) 646-0111
Website
- www.nmsu.edu
Admission Fee
- None
Directions
- Drive west on I-10 toward Las Cruces, then drive north on I-25. Take Exit 1 in Las Cruces, and turn left at the stop sign onto University Road. Cross the overpass. As a visitor, you are allowed to park anywhere on campus after 4:30 or on weekends. If you wish to visit during the day, you can get a free visitor's pass to park anywhere on campus by e-mailing NMSU at parking@nmsu.edu. You may also park in lots known as "Free Lots," located on the eastern side of the Pan American building near I-25.

The Walks

Dogs will enjoy the easy trotting found along the lined pathways and sloping lawns across the New Mexico State grounds. The School of Agriculture on the northwest side of campus maintains horses, cows, and other animals. Avoid this section of campus if your dog is likely to bark or growl at livestock, making them nervous.

Dog Friendliness

What is a college campus without dogs on the lawn?

Traffic

There are few more pleasant dogwalking expereinces than
NMSU when classes are not in session. During the fall and spring
semesters, the campus is a bustling place.

Canine Swimming

Ornamental ponds stocked with goldfish grace the campus but
dogs should be kept to the shoreline.

Trail Time

Less than an hour.

*"If you pick up a starving dog and make him prosperous,
he will not bite you; that is the principal
difference between a dog and a man."*
- Mark Twain

26

University of Texas at El Paso

The Campus

The park-like university campus is one of the desert southwest's most beautiful, replete with benches and cacti, sage and other plants that burst into bloom in late May and August. UTEP features the largest collection of Bhutanese architecture in the western hemisphere. In 1917, after the original Texas State School of Mines and Metallurgy buildings burned to the ground, construction began on the new campus, which is today the University of Texas at El Paso.

City of El Paso
Difficulty Rating - 1
Phone Number - (915) 747-5000
Website - www.utep.edu
Admission Fee - None
Directions - From I-10, take the Schuster/UTEP exit. UTEP is at the end of the ramp heading west and under the overpass heading east. You can park anywhere on campus before 7 a.m. and after 5 p.m. on weekdays, and all day on weekends or when school is not in session.

Kathleen L. Worrell, wife of the first dean, suggested that the new buildings be modeled after Bhutanese architecture she remembered from the April 1914 *The National Geographic*. Architects used photographs from the magazine as their guide to bringing the feel of the remote Himalayan kingdom of Bhutan to the Franklin Mountains. Old Main is one of the purest pieces of Bhutanese architecture on campus, with sloping walls, over-hanging hip roof, windows set deep into the thick walls, off-white stucco finish, and a broad red-brick-and-mosaic band between the upper story windows.

The Walks

UTEP is a commuter campus and dogwalking is a quiet affair when class is not in session. The campus is set in the foothills of the Franklin Mountains, so there are a few hills and patches of desert that allow you to get away from the buildings and concrete. This is particularly true to the west of Sun Bowl Drive.

Dog Friendliness

Dogs are welcome, though required to be on leashes.

Traffic

You and the dog can expect a solitary walk around campus when school is not in session.

Canine Swimming

None.

Trail Time

Less than an hour.

"Children are for people who can't have dogs."
- Anonymous

27

Tortugas Mountain

The Park

The Tortugas Pueblo Indians give great spiritual significance to Tortugas Mountain, giving it a central role in the annual celebration to honor the Virgin of Guadalupe, Mexico's patron saint. It is believed that the Virgin of Guadalupe appeared to the Indian Juan Diego (canonized on July 31, 2002) in 1531 outside of Mexico City. The Virgin Mary's appearance was significant because she appeared to an Indian and because she appeared as a dark woman with Indian features. This legitimized Catholicism to Indians, who subsequently converted, thus making Mexico a Catholic country. Each year, on December 10, the Tortugas Pueblo Indians stage a three-day ceremony of dancing, feasting, and worship to honor the Virgin. The celebration begins with costumes, dancing, and shotgun blasts to ward off evil spirits. The next day, pilgrims gather to form a procession, carrying the image of the Virgin four miles to the top of Tortugas Mountain. The ceremony ends on December 12 with a high mass and a feast in the afternoon.

City of Las Cruces

Difficulty Rating
- 2
Phone Number
- (505) 438-7542
Website
- www.nm.blm.gov/www/
new_home_2.html
Admission Fee
- None
Directions
- From I-10, drive north to Las Cruces and take I-25 north toward Albuquerque. Take exit 1 to University Ave. At the stop sign, turn right toward the mountains. Follow this road, which curves and dips, and eventually becomes a dirt road, until you reach a large hill that has a capital letter "A" written on it in white rocks. Park on the side of the road.

The Walks

This hike can be laid back or strenuous, depending on how you and your dog decide to ascend the mountain (which is more like a hill). A circuitous route zig-zags lazily up Tortugas Mountain and an alternative route runs straight to the top. The trail can be steep and a little slippery, so watch your footing. The mountain can also be circled around the base. People occasionally shoot cans and bottles with rifles or shotguns here, so watch for broken glass that a dogs could get in her paws.

Dog Friendliness

This is a great area to take dogs and let them run free.

Traffic

People do bring their dogs to walk up Tortugas Mountain but there is plenty of room for everyone.

Canine Swimming

None.

Trail Time

More than an hour.

28

Black Mountain

The Park

Black Mountain is a cinder cone volcano, rising 4,502 feet out of the flat desert mesa with several tall dunes lying adjacent to it. Many homeowners in the Southwest use black lava rock in their front yards, rather than struggling to grow grass. Black Mountain is one of the sites where this black lava rock is mined.

The Walks

You can follow the road directly into the volcano, climb one of the dunes, or head out into the desert. The dunes adjacent to Black Mountain and the surrounding desert are relatively free of black volcanic rock; the road becomes progressively riddled with black rock as it heads into the volcano. You might want to limit the amount of time you spend in the volcano for the sake of your dog's paws, and spend more time on the dunes or in the desert. Views of the mountains: the Franklins, the Organs, and the San Andres, are spectacular from here.

Doña Ana County

Difficulty Rating
- 2
Phone Number
- (505) 438-7542
Website
- www.nm.blm.gov/www/ new_home_2.html
Admission Fee
- None
Directions
- From I-10, head west toward Las Cruces. Exit at the Anthony exit (Exit 0). Turn right and follow the street until it intersects with Main Street in Anthony. Turn right onto Main Street. A quarter mile later, turn left onto Highway 478 and drive to Berino, New Mexico. Take a left onto NM 226 in Berino and follow this road 2.5 miles, which will end at a T with Highway 28. Go right and follow the road 1.5 miles until you come to an intersection at Afton Rd. Turn left. Follow Afton Road for 5.7 miles. As you near Black Mountain on the left, turn left onto the dirt road at the intersection. Drive 2 miles and park the car. Do not drive into the volcano where your car could get stuck.

Dog Friendliness

Dogs are permitted throughout this land, managed by the BLM.

Traffic

During the week, keep your dog clear of trucks and workers carting away the decorative black rock. On weekends you may not see anyone, save a stray geologist here and there.

Canine Swimming

None.

Trail Time

More than an hour.

"No one appreciates the very special genius
of your conversation as a dog does."
- Christopher Morley

29

Oliver Lee State Park

The Park

Oliver Lee State Park is the legacy to Oliver Milton Lee (1865-1941), an American pioneer who staked out a ranch at the mouth of Dog Canyon. Lee became noted in the area as the accused murderer of A.J. Fountain and his young son. Fountain, chief prosecutor for the Southeastern New Mexico Stock Growers Association, angered Lee by securing indictments against him for cattle rustling. Lee was charged with Fountain's murder in 1896 but was acquitted, partly because Fountain's body was never found.

The Walks

Dog Canyon is a six-mile one way trek into the Lincoln Forest, rising from an elevation of about 4,000 feet to about 7,000 feet, from the desert to the beginning of pine forests. The trail is steep in places, then levels off before concluding with one last challenging climb. For dogs not up to the full adventure, an old cabin marks a convenient turning-around spot at the halfway point. The trail is well-marked and easy to follow, but strenuous.

Dog Friendliness

Dogs are permitted on the trails in Oliver Lee State Park.

Otero County

Difficulty Rating
 - 2
Phone Number
 - (505) 437-8284
Website
 - www.emnrd.state.nm.us/
 nmparks/PAGES/PARKS/
 OLIVER/OLIVER.HTM
Admission Fee
 - $4 per vehicle
Directions
 - From El Paso, take I-54 north towards Alamogordo. About ten miles before Alamogordo, turn right onto Dog Canyon Road at the sign indicating the turnoff for Oliver Lee State Park. Drive 4 miles to reach the park.
 - From Las Cruces, take I-70 towards Alamogordo and pick up I-54 toward El Paso. Drive 10 miles to Dog Canyon Road and turn left at the sign for Oliver Lee State Park. Turn left and drive 4 miles to the park.

Traffic

The trails at Oliver Lee are popular in the spring and fall, especially on the weekends.

Canine Swimming

None.

Trail Time

More than an hour.

"Ever consider what they must think of us?
I mean, here we come back from the grocery store
with the most amazing haul - chicken, pork,
half a cow...They must think we're the
greatest hunters on earth!"
- Anne Tyler

30

Chamizal National Memorial

The Park

Chamizal National Memorial is a symbol of goodwill between the United States and Mexico, a healing between two nations over a dispute of land. When the boundary between the U.S. and Mexico was set at the Rio Grande, nobody realized that the river would shift its course late in the 19th century. A large chunk of Mexican land slowly shifted until it came to rest inside American boundaries. A Mexican citizen named Pedro I. Garcia filed suit for the return of 7.82 acres in 1895 and began a controversy that lasted for sixty-eight years. Early in the twentieth century, an arbitration committee ruled in favor of Mexico, but the United States rejected the decision. Muted tension lasted until 1963, when the United States ceded several hundred acres to Mexico as part of the Chamizal Treaty. The river had to be directed in its course by concrete canals. With the issue finally resolved, each nation created a memorial park on its side of the river as a gesture of good will.

City of El Paso

Difficulty Rating
- 1
Phone Number
- (915) 532-7273
Website
- None
Admission Fee
- None
Directions
- From I-10 heading east, take exit 22B near the I-10/I-54 interchange known as the Spaghetti Bowl. Follow the brown signs pointing toward the Chamizal. (Be careful not to go towards Juárez.) Take a right at the Y onto Paisano. At the first light, San Marcial St., take a left.

The Walks

Chamizal National Memorial, with its lined paths, grassy patches, and trees, provides a refreshing contrast to much of desert landscaped El Paso. From here, you can watch traffic cross into Mexico on the free bridge. The park's easy-to-follow trail provides a great panorama of the Franklin Mountains.

Bonus

**The mural painted on the outside wall of the Chamizal,
one of the better preserved murals in the city, is a fine
representative of Chicano/Hispanic art. It depicts the
historical blending of cultures along the U.S./Mexico
Border and is aptly named "Nuestra Herencia" or
"Our Heritage." It also honors the presidential leaders who
solved the land issue between Mexico and the United
States when the Rio Grande shifted course.**

Dog Friendliness

Dogs are welcome except on Sunday nights during the summer, when the park offers concerts.

Traffic

People like to walk here, so bring dogs on their best behavior to these paths.

Canine Swimming

None.

Trail Time

Less than an hour.

31

Arroyo Park

The Park

Arroyos can be as small as a ditch or as wide as a canyon, but no matter how small or big, they all provide the same function: transporting water from the mountain to the valley below when it rains. Arroyos are important sources of water in mountainous desert regions, so they are a good place to watch for wildlife and birds. Arroyos are also a good spot to look for vegetation that will not grow in the drier areas of the basin or mesa. In the spring, keep your eye out for wildflowers.

City of El Paso

Difficulty Rating
- 1-2
Phone Number
- None
Website
- crl.nmsu.edu/~mleisher/bmba/ MonksArroyoPark.jpg (*trail map*)
Admission Fee
- None
Directions
- From I-10, take the Schuster/ UTEP exit, and follow Schuster east toward the Franklin Mountains. Turn left on Mesa, then right on Kerbey. Follow Kerby to Virginia and turn right. Follow Virginia a quarter mile and you will have reached the lower part of the park.

The Walks

Trails criss-cross through this old arroyo, and you can meander at leisure. Although arroyos can be sandy, so many people walk this trail every day that the trail is hard-packed and easy to walk. Despite the fact this is the desert, the trails are so well-traversed you don't need to worry about stickers in paws.

Warning: If it is raining in the mountains, do not go hiking in arroyos. They are channels for rainwater coming off the mountain, and they can fill up with several feet of rushing water within seconds.

Dog Friendliness

This is a popular place to bring dogs.

Traffic

Expect mountain bikers and fellow canine hikers along these desert trails.

Canine Swimming

No.

Trail Time

Less than an hour.

*"I can't think of anything that brings me closer to tears than
when my old dog - completely exhausted after a hard day
in the field - limps away from her nice spot in front of the fire and
comes over to where I'm sitting and puts her head in my lap,
a paw over my knee, and closes her eyes, and goes back to sleep.
I don't know what I've done to deserve that kind of friend."*
- Gene Hill

32

Pancho Villa State Park

The Park

In the early morning hours of March 9, 1916, Mexican revolutionary Pancho Villa and 500 men raided the tiny border town of Columbus and killed 18 Americans. The audacious attack was the first hostile invasion of the United States since the War of 1812. General John "Black Jack" Pershing led a retaliatory expedition deep into Mexico to hunt Villa down and return him to the United States for justice. The Punitive Expedition, 10,000 soldiers strong, returned after 11 months empty-handed. Pancho Villa State Park was created in 1959 as a gesture of goodwill between the United States and Mexico. Seven years later, in 1966, Praxedes Giner Duran, governor of Chihuahua, dedicated the "avenida de Amistad" (Avenue of Friendship) and presented 400 sycamores to the state of New Mexico. Geologically, the park lies on the edge of a large alluvial fan that extends southeast from the Tres Hermanas Mountains, which lie five miles to the northwest, and were mined until the 1920s for zinc, silver, gold, lead, and copper.

Town of Columbus

Difficulty Rating
- 1
Phone Number
- (505) 531-2711
Website
- www.emnrd.state.nm.us/nmparks/PAGES/PARKS/PANCHO/PANCHO.HTM
Admission Fee
- $4 per vehicle
Directions
- From I-10, take the Artcraft Road exit in El Paso. Turn west, away from the mountains, and continue on Texas 178, which turns into South 136 in New Mexico. Follow this until you see signs directing you to turn onto Highway 9 towards Columbus, New Mexico. About sixty-six miles from the I-10 turnoff, you will reach Columbus. The State Park is located just beyond the Highway 9 and 11 intersection in Columbus.

The Walks

The 60-acre park features a short and easy nature trail that highlights area cacti. The botanical garden is outstanding with more than 30 different species of desert plants, including ocotillo, yucca and agave, mesquite, purple cholla, snowball cactus, polka dot cactus, barrel cactus, stag horn cholla, snowball cactus, and jubilee trees. Also in the park is a one-mile exercise loop trail that weaves through picnic tables.

Dog Friendliness

Dogs are welcome, though they should be leashed. Watch out for the cactus, which proliferates off the path.

Traffic

The coolest time to visit the park is October through March, when most of the people, dogs and birds come.

Canine Swimming

None.

Trail Time

Less than an hour.

33

Alameda Arroyo & Tortugas Arroyo

The Arroyos

Arroyos are an important waterway in the desert, and as a result, wildlife is attracted to them. Plants grow more easily here than on the flat mesa or along rocky mountain ridges. Walking inside an arroyo can be like slipping into another world, hidden from sight. Among an arroyo's treasures is the desert willow, which is not a willow at all, although it resembles the tree and sprouts beautiful orchid-shaped flowers. Although desert willows can survive in a wide range of habitats, they show a preference for the damper soil of washes and arroyos. Desert willows flower in the late spring and during the summer.

The Walks

Arroyos can be friendlier to dogs than humans. They may be sandy, soft on a dog's paws and easy to traverse.

Doña Ana County

Difficulty Rating
- 2
Phone Number
- (505) 438-7542
Website
- www.nm.blm.gov/www/new_home_2.html
Admission Fee
- None
Directions
- *Alameda Arroyo:* From El Paso, take I-10 west. In Las Cruces, take I-25 north, then turn onto Route 70 towards Alamogordo. Go 11 miles, turn right onto Baylor Canyon Road. Drive 4.6 miles to the Alameda Arroyo.
Tortugas Arroyo: From El Paso, take I-10 west towards Deming. In Las Cruces, take Exit 142 and turn left onto University Avenue. Go under the overpass and take an immediate left on Main Street (Highway 478). A short distance later, turn left onto East Union Drive. Just before crossing under the freeway, turn right on Stern Drive, the frontage road. One mile later, at Salopek Boulevard, the arroyo will be directly in front of you. Pull into the dirt parking lot on the left of Salopek, near the park.

When humans may turn an ankle in stony spots, dogs will have fun with the hidden crevasses and twists and turns. Both of these arroyos are sandy in spots and rocky in others. Watch your step and enjoy along with your dog!

Dog Friendliness
Arroyos are great places to bring dogs. Arroyos are important sources of water and wildlife tends to congregate here so dogs that revel in chasing jackrabbits will find lots of tail-wagging fun here.

Traffic
Tortugas Arroyo attracts some 3-wheelers, but most of the time you can expect a solitary walk. Geologists and biologists visit occasionally on field trips.

Canine Swimming
None.

Trail Time
More than an hour.

34

Aden Crater

The Crater

Aden Crater, part of the Potrillo volcanic field, lies directly above the Robledo Fault line. Aden Crater formed in five stages. Initially, lava flows built a shield cone, with gentle slopes that dipped away from the center. This was followed by a more explosive phase when spatter, ejected from the volcano, created a circular rim around the surface. A rift in the southern part of the crater produced several small spatter cones nearby. In the next stage, lava rose to the surface but was prevented from overflowing by the circular rim, creating a lava lake. In the next stage, the center of the main crater collapsed, leaving what you see today. Finally, a fumerole, a ground vent that emits only gases, formed on the east rim.

The Walks

Aden Crater is the size of a football stadium and the surrounding desert stretches for miles. Your dog can run until he tuckers out. Though this is a great place to take

Doña Ana County

Difficulty Rating
- 3 (leans toward a 4)
Phone Number
- (505) 438-7542
Website
- www.nm.blm.gov/www/ new_home_2.html
Admission Fee
- None
Directions
- From I-10, take Vinton/ Westway exit (exit #2). Going west, turn left onto Vinton Road. Going east, turn right onto Vinton Road. Go 1.8 miles, across Doniphan Road and the Rio Grande. At the Y, turn left onto North Vinton Road and follow it 2 miles to State Highway 28, and make another left. Make an immediate right onto Mercantil Road, which is also State Highway 182 West. When the road forks less than a mile ahead, take the right fork and follow it .1 miles to Alvarez Road, and turn right. Alvarez road turns into a dirt road. At the next fork, take the left fork. This dirt road becomes County Rd. A-20. Follow it 6.7 miles, past the railroad tracks, to a T in the road, and turn right. Follow this road for 29 miles (you will cross the lava flows twice), take one of the unmarked primitive roads left and follow it around the right side of the lava flows. Park your car when you see the volcano to your front left as you park your car.

dogs, don't spend too much time walking on the lava flow areas, where the rough rock (which forms part of the ground surface) can be tough on your dog's paws.

Dog Friendliness

Aden Crater, like other places on the West Mesa, provides solitude and lots of space. You can let your dog run free, but watch for rattlesnakes and coyotes. It is still wild out here.

Traffic

On occasion, you may run into a geologist or two, out to see one of the Southwest's most spectacular volcano craters. But you can generally expect to be alone. Because of this, take plenty of water and a cell phone.

Canine Swimming

None.

Trail Time

More than an hour.

"Scratch a dog and you'll find a permanent job."
- Franklin P. Jones

35

Mt. Riley

The Mountain

Rising 5,905 feet from the mesa floor in a dome shape, Mt. Riley has long played a role in local mythology. In one tall tale, a retired soldier found a boulder rolled over a cave entrance. When he displaced the rock, he found a cave of mummified Indians with all their goods inside. He pushed the rock back into place and went to tell people of his find, but the cave has never been located again. In another tale, people claim that camels used in a failed army experiment escaped from Ft. Furlong in 1900. The lost dromedaries supposedly survived, and possibly bred, in these mountains. Mt. Riley is volcanic in origin but sports small outcrops of marine limestone on the side slopes.

The Walks

The ascent of Mt. Riley is strenuous, about seven miles both ways. The trail is not marked, and areas of loose rock on the eastern slope demand caution. To reach the base of

Doña Ana County

Difficulty Rating
  - 3
Phone Number
  - (505) 438-7542
Website
  - www.nm.blm.gov/www/
    new_home_2.html
Admission Fee
  - None
Directions
  - From I-10, turn off on the Vinton/Westway exit (exit #2). Going west, turn left onto Vinton Road. Going east, turn right onto Vinton Road. Follow it 1.8 miles, across Doniphan Road and the Rio Grande. At the Y, turn left onto North Vinton Road and follow it 2 miles to State Highway 28, and make another left. Make an immediate right onto Mercantil Road (State Highway 182 West). The road forks less than a mile ahead. Take the right fork for 1/10 of a mile to Alvarez Road, and turn right. Alvarez Road turns into a dirt road; take the left road at the next fork which becomes County Rd. A-20. Follow it 6.7 miles, past the railroad tracks, to a "T" in the road, and turn right. About .5 of a mile later, turn left onto County Road A-14. Follow this road west 13.3 miles to a stop sign. Turn right and go 1 mile before turning north again. Go .7 mile, turn left onto County Road A-10 for 1.3 miles. Turn left and travel 3.5 miles southwest to Gap Tank and park.

the peak, hike northwest along the arroyo for about 1/4 mile, then hike west across the mesa for about a mile. Your reward at the top is splendid views across the region's mountains.

Dog Friendliness

The freedom, space, and solitude of Mt. Riley make this a great place to take dogs.

Canine Swimming

None.

Traffic

This is as desolate as it gets. Bring plenty of water, a cell phone, a first aid kit, and make sure your spare tire is inflated.

Trail Time

More than an hour.

36
Caballo Mountains

The Trail

The passage through the Caballo Mountains was part of Juan de Oñate's El Camino Real (The Royal Road), which he traveled from Mexico City to Santa Fe in search for gold in 1598 with 83 wheeled oxcarts and several thousand head of cattle. However, his provisions and cattle were no match for the Jornada del Muerto (the Journey of Death), the long stretch of desert that begins on the northeastern side of the Caballos. Half his cattle and a third of his men perished before Piro Pueblo Indians rescued him. The mountains have long been visited by treasure seekers chasing Spanish gold that was rumored to be buried here.

Sierra County

Difficulty Rating
- 4
Phone Number
- (505) 438-7542
Website
- www.nm.blm.gov/www/ new_home_2.html
Admission Fee
- None
Directions
- From Las Cruces, drive north on I-25 to Truth or Consequences. Take Exit 75 and drive through town until you reach the only stop light, Third Street. Turn right on Third Street and drive until you reach the Rio Grande. Cross the bridge and turn right immediately after crossing. Follow the river downstream along this dirt road for approximately five miles until you pass a ranch and reach a gate. Drive through the gate and park or, if you have an off-road vehicle, go until you want to stop and hike.

The Walks

Hikes in the Caballo Mountains follow jeep trails, arroyos, canyons, and small trails scattered here and there. It requires an intrepid soul to bring dogs into this very undeveloped land, and though it may take some time and perseverance, the Caballo Mountains are worth it for their solitude and quiet desert beauty.

Dog Friendliness

Like the Floridas, the Sierra de las Uvas, and the Robledos, the Caballo Mountains are rugged and wild. On the one hand, this means your dog can roam off the leash without fear of disturbing anybody. On the other hand, you do need to keep an eye out for snakes and small mammals.

Traffic

Few people travel or hike in the Caballos because they are not easily accessible.

Canine Swimming

None.

Trail Time

More than an hour.

37
Artcraft Road Trail

The Trail

Unlike many other cities in the west, El Paso makes few accommodations for walkers and bike-riders. Artcraft Road Trail is an attempt to create more city trails. The city-maintained trail ends promptly and judiciously at the New Mexico State Line.

The Walks

This is a well-maintained biking/walking path in a rural setting with great views of the Franklin Mountains to the east and Mt. Cristo Rey and the

City of El Paso

Difficulty Rating
- 1
Phone Number
- None
Website
- None
Admission Fee
- None
Directions
- From I-10, take the Artcraft Road exit and turn west away from the mountains. You can park near the canal at the Upper Valley Road or the Westside intersection, or you can keep driving and park at the Texas State Line sign where the bicycle and walking trail ends.

Juárez Mountains to the south. Under the bridge is a great place to take off for another hike along the Rio Grande and hikeable irrigation canals also radiate off the main trail. Artcraft Road Trail weaves through irrigated farmland of chile, cotton, corn and alfalfa; mosquitoes appear promptly at dusk.

Dog Friendliness

This trail is perfect for a quick jaunt with your dog, but it does run parallel to a busy street, so it is important to keep your dog on the leash.

Traffic

This is a popular trail you will share with other dog-walkers, joggers, strollers, bikers, and skaters.

Canine Swimming

The trail intersects with the river, but I don't recommend letting dogs swim in the Rio Grande this far south unless your dog has a gut of steel. (Only a few miles up the road, however, the Rio Grande is a great canine swimming hole.)

Trail Time

More than an hour.

38

Keystone Heritage Park

The Park

Much of this land was once owned by Zach White, an El Paso rancher who arrived in 1881 with $10,000 sewn into the back of his vest. He sold groceries at first, but moved on to hardware, brick manufacturing, and real estate over the next 40 years. Among his other contributions, White donated the land for the El Paso Country Club. In 1979-1980, archeologists were called in to determine the site of an ancient American Indian village, built between 3600-4800 years ago, and a dam was built to avoid covering the area with water. Nearly 40 houses may be contained at the site, which is the largest collection of Archaic-period houses in the United States. It is also the oldest known village in the West. Located on the east side of the dam, Keystone Heritage Park is a desert wetlands-in-progress.

City of El Paso

Difficulty Rating
- 1
Phone Number
- (915) 584-0563
Website
- www.KeystonePark.com
Admission Fee
- None
Directions
- From I-10, take the Sunland Park exit. If traveling west, turn left. If traveling east, turn right. Take a right at the first stoplight, Doniphan Road. Exactly .5 mile later, turn right on an unmarked paved road. Keystone Heritage Park is to your immediate left. Drive left off the paved road and park. Walk north an eighth of a mile to reach the pond.

The Walks

The 52 acres of desert wetlands provide about three miles of walking if you traverse the side of the lake/pond, then proceed to climb the dam and walk along its ridge. The walk is not difficult and there is no trail because there are few shrubs or trees except against the dam. Though the land here is not spectacularly beautiful, it has great views of Mt. Franklin.

Dog Friendliness

Dogs are welcome here, but if you're walking near the wetlands, they should remain on their leashes so they don't scare the birds. Up on the dam, you may let them off the leash.

Traffic

This is a popular spot for walking dogs.

Canine Swimming

None.

Trail Time

Less than an hour.

"If you don't think dogs can count,
try putting three dog biscuits in your pocket
and giving Fido two."

- Phil Pastoret

39
Via de la Paz Trail

The Trail

This paved hiking path begins off Via de la Paz. Heading west, it rambles alongside a paved arroyo. Heading east, it quickly becomes a gravel track reaching into the Franklin Mountains. The paved part of the trail is maintained by the City of El Paso. The unpaved, mountainous trails are ostensibly part of Franklin Mountain State Park, though the trails are not maintained, nor are they part of the fee structure that you find in other parts of the state park.

The Walks

This is an easy hike on a clearly-marked path. If you wander onto one of the numerous narrow and steep mountain bike trails, you will find the trail is more strenuous and you are more likely to brush up against a cactus.

Dog Friendliness

Dogs are welcome on the trail.

Traffic

This is a popular trail for dog-walkers. Vehicular traffic continues with mountain bikers on the unpaved trails.

El Paso County

Difficulty Rating
- 2
Phone Number
- None
Website
- None
Admission Fee
- None
Directions
- From I-10, take the Sunland Park exit. If driving west, turn right. If driving east, turn left. Take Sunland Park Road east towards the mountains. The road becomes Shadow Mountain after a mile, then becomes Westwind Road after another mile. Drive until you reach Belvidere Road. Turn right toward the mountain and drive 1.4 miles, past the Monte Vista nursing home. Turn left on a street called Via Monte. Turn right on Via Loma. Turn left on Via de la Paz. Park on Los Pueblos, .1 mile later.

Canine Swimming

None.

Trail Time

More than an hour.

Prickly pear cactus and desert yucca decorate the Via de la Paz Trail.

40
Memorial Park

The Campus

Memorial Park is an old smelter site. The remains of slag dumps were finally cleaned up in the 1930s, when the WPA transformed the area into a park. Streets in this neighborhood, "Manhattan Heights," were named as a tip of the hat to the original use of the property - Copper, Silver, Gold, Bronze, etc. The neighborhood of small bungalow and Spanish Colonial Revival houses is unique, built by El Paso's first female architect, Mabel Welch.

City of El Paso

Difficulty Rating
- 1
Phone Number
- None
Website
- None
Admission Fee
- None
Directions
- Take I-10 to the Piedras exit in central El Paso. Coming from the west, turn left onto Piedras Street and go under the freeway. Coming from the east, turn right onto Piedras. Drive past Montana Street and Pershing Street. Turn right onto Copper Street, which ends at the park.

The Walks

Memorial Park is hilly, with wide paths and lots of trees; it is a good place to meander in the company of songbirds and mourning doves. Definitely not flat walking, but nothing strenuous.

Dog Friendliness

Dogs are welcome, although they should remain on a leash.

Traffic

Memorial Park is a popular spot to bring the dog.

Canine Swimming

None.

Trail Time

Less than an hour.

"A door is what a dog is perpetually on the wrong side of."
- James Thurber

41

Wilderness Park Museum Nature Trail

The Museum & Trail

The Wilderness Park Museum educates El Paso area schoolchildren about Native Americans in the Southwest and northern Mexico, as well as to providing information about how humans have interacted with the Chihuahuan Desert environment. (The Border Patrol History Museum is located next door, and the Nature Trail skirts around it. If you're interested in the history of the U.S. Border Patrol, it is worth a visit, although dogs are not allowed inside.)

City of El Paso

Difficulty Rating
- 1
Phone Number
- (915) 755-4332
Website
- None
Admission Fee
- Donations
Directions
- The Wilderness Park Museum of El Paso is located at 4301 Transmountain, on the northeast side of the Franklin Mountains. Transmountain can be accessed via I-10 on the Westside or via the Patriot Freeway in the Northeast.

The Walks

Despite its short length, the nature hike provides a unique glimpse of the Chihuahuan Desert wilderness, with many of the more than 200 native plants identified by signs. The trail is easy to follow but does not provide a lot of canine exercise.

Beyond the Wilderness Park, the Franklin Mountains extend northward in the Castner Range, once a shooting range for Ft. Bliss. There is no danger on the Wilderness Park Nature Trail or near it, but you should avoid walking in the Castner Range itself. Many people do it, but unexploded shells are lying around, and if you are caught, you will be fined.

Dog Friendliness

Dogs should be on their leashes at all times.

Traffic

Expect to run into foot traffic on this trail.

Canine Swimming

None.

Trail Time

Less than an hour.

"A watchdog is a dog kept to guard the house,
usually by sleeping where a burglar
would awaken the house by falling over him."
- Anonymous

42
Redd Road Trail

The Trail

The desert beyond Redd Road tickles the boundary of Franklin Mountain State Park but is not an official park. It is a great place to go hiking in the desert now, although it is subject to development and may disappear in a few years as the city grows. People who buy these houses have access to public lands, and may be able to prevent its use. In the meantime, as long as there is access, enjoy it.

City of El Paso

Difficulty Rating
 - 2
Phone Number
 - None
Website
 - None
Admission Fee
 - None
Directions
 - From I-10, heading toward Las Cruces, take the Redd Road exit. Turn right (east) toward the Franklin Mountains, and follow the road until it dead-ends.

The Walks

Bike paths and walking trails criss-cross, forming miles of trailscape that eventually combine with the Via de la Paz trail to the south. Follow whatever trail strikes your fancy. Many lead straight to the base of the mountain near Transmountain Road, while others traipse north across the mesa and foothills. Eventually, most paths will dead-end at Transmountain Road.

Dog Friendliness

There are no prohibitions against dogs in this undeveloped desert.

Traffic

These convenient trails are dominated by mountain bikers, especially on weekends and holidays. Keep a close rein on your dog.

Bonus

The creosote bush, which can be seen everywhere from the Redd Road Trail, is not native to the Chihuahua Desert. It arrived 4000 years ago, moving north from the tropics of South America and settling along the border regions and parts of the Southwest. However, it did not spread rapidly until over-grazing led to desertification. Creosote bushes survive well in desert climates. During drought, the leaves shrivel, but the bush survives. During rain, its shallow roots thirstily absorb the water from the surrounding soil, leaching it of moisture that other plants need to grow. American Indians make use of the plant in many ways, including to make glue and brew tea. It was used as pain medication for menstrual cramps, and brewed together with milkweed to draw out the poison from snake bites.

Canine Swimming

None.

Trail Time

More than an hour.

A trail leads into the Franklin Mountains.

43

Concordia Cemetery

The Cemetery

Hugh Stephenson and his wife Juana Maria Ascarate, two leading citizens of El Paso, constructed a hacienda here during the 1840s. Both a chapel and a cemetery rose on the property in 1854. When Mrs. Stephenson was gored by a pet deer in 1856, she became the first person to be buried in Concordia Cemetery. During the Civil War, the Stephenson ranch was destroyed and Ft. Bliss occupied the site for a few years. Stephenson lost the property after the war, but his son-in-law reacquired it in 1867, selling equal portions of the ranch to Stephenson heirs for a dollar apiece. In the 1880s, civic pressure led to the creation of the cemetery. The City of El Paso bought its first share of the cemetery in 1882 as a gravesite for paupers. Different groups bought shares of the property and the cemetery was divided into various segregated sections: Jewish, Black, Masonic, Chinese. There is even a section devoted to the black Buffalo Soldiers who died here while serving in the U.S. Army. Today, there are approximately 65,000 graves in Concordia Cemetery.

City of El Paso

Difficulty Rating
- 1
Phone Number
- (915) 562-7062
Website
- None
Admission Fee
- None
Directions
- From I-10 near the I-54 interchange, take the Copia Street exit. Turn north on Copia. (Driving east on I-10, turn left and go under the freeway. Driving west, turn right.) A few blocks later, turn right on Yandell Street. The cemetery is on the right.

The Walks

The cemetery consists of both privately and publicly owned land, and nobody assumes responsibility for the upkeep. Thus, certain sections are kept repaired and are pleasant to walk in, and other sections are in disrepair and need a lot of work. The walk is

122

not strenuous, and there are plenty of paths among the graves, which are not always well-marked.

Dog Friendliness

The Concordia Heritage Association welcomes anyone to the cemetery who wants to learn about El Paso's early history and dogs are permitted to tag along. This is a precious historical resource so keep your dog on the leash, stay on the paths (except when visiting gravesites), and clean up after your dogs.

Traffic

Your canine hike in Concordia Cemetery is likely to be a peaceful one.

Canine Swimming

None.

Trail Time

Less than an hour.

44
Mt. Cristo Rey

The Mountain

The cross on the top of Mt. Cristo Rey represents the spot where two countries and three states meet - Mexico and the U.S., and the states of Texas, New Mexico, and Chihuahua (although the actual meeting site is in the river below). Half of Mt. Cristo Rey (the half with a hiking trail) belongs to the U.S.; the other half belongs to Mexico. The north half of the mountain, like all of southern New Mexico, became part of the United States in the Treaty of Guadalupe Hidalgo, which ended the Mexican-American War in 1848. In need of money, Mexican General Antonio López de Santa Anna capitulated to American demands and accepted $10,000,000 for a slice of land extending from western Arizona to West Texas, a real estate deal known as the Gadsden Purchase. In El Paso, Mexican troops had declared they would defend their soil against invading Americans, but backed down when presented with a certified copy of General Santa Anna's order to surrender the purchased territory. Overnight, 75,000 Spanish-speaking inhabitants became American citizens. Today, the Gadsden Purchase, completed in 1853, is still remembered by Mexicans as one of Mexico's most humiliating moments.

Doña Ana County

Difficulty Rating
 - 2
Phone Number
 - None
Website
 - None
Admission Fee
 - None
Directions
 - From I-10, take the Mesa-Executive exit and turn west toward the ASARCO smelter and Mt. Cristo Rey. Turn right on Paisano. A mile later, exit on HW 273 South. .5 mile later, turn left at the green historical marker that points to the road leading up to the mountain.

The Walks

There is just one path, which curves in and around the hills, meandering up to the cross at the top of the mountain. It is steep and, at times, slippery, but it provides great views of the west side of El Paso. The hike is frequently made as a religious pilgrimage and fourteen small white crosses mark the Stations of the Cross along the way.

Dog Friendliness

Dogs are welcome on the mountain and there is no need for a leash.

Traffic

Except for holy pilgrimages at Easter and on the feast day of the Virgin of Guadalupe, few people visit Mt. Cristo Rey. You might run into one or two other people. However, it is locally notorious as a hiding place for bandits. Warning signs advise not to leave valuables in the car and to travel in groups when possible.

Canine Swimming

None.

Trail Time

More than an hour.

45

Three Hills Park

The Park

Three Hills is a neighborhood park, creating a sort of vast "backyard desert" for a number of houses. The city has failed to designate it as a park with   signs or give it a parking space. Currently, a church is erecting a new building next to the park, further inhibiting access. However, it is worth being persistent, as the park provides splendid views of El Paso's Westside and the farming valley.

The Walks

The three hills are steep and paths tend to go straight up, so the hike is short but sporty. There's not much brush or growth on the slopes, however, so it is not necessary to follow the paths. The hills are rocky and stony so be careful, as they can be slippery under paw. The nearby dam is off-limits, and signs warn you to keep away.

Dog Friendliness

As in all city parks, dogs are welcome here.

Traffic

You will probably run into one or two people on this hike.

City of El Paso

Difficulty Rating
- 2
Phone Number
- None
Website
- None
Admission Fee
- None
Directions
- In El Paso, take I-10 west (toward Las Cruces) and exit on Redd Road. Turn right and follow Redd Road to Resler Road. You will pass the park on your left just before you reach Resler, but there is no available parking. Turn left on Resler and park in the shopping center to your left. You must backtrack on foot to the park.

Canine Swimming

None.

Trail Time

Less than an hour.

"To err is human, to forgive, canine."
- Anonymous

No Dogs!

Feather Lake Bird Sanctuary
(City of El Paso)
Call (915) 757-1876 or 915-545-5157 for more information.

Hueco Tanks State Park
(El Paso County)
Call (915) 857-1135 for more information.

Dripping Springs and La Cueva Picnic Area
(Las Cruces)
For more information, call the BLM at (505) 525-4300.

Guadalupe Mountains National Park
(west Texas)
For more information, call (915) 828-3251.

Three Rivers Petroglyph Site
(southern New Mexico)
(Dogs are allowed in the campground, but not on the trails.)
Call (505) 585-3458 for more information.

San Andres National Wildlife Refuge
(No dogs and no people unless you're a volunteer.)
Call 505/382-5047 for more information.

City Parks...

El Paso

Eastwood Album Park
A crowded park, near a crowded street, but it is tree-lined and provides a pleasant place to walk your dog if you can find a time to avoid the crowds.

Edgemere Park
Edgemere is a long, slender open space where you can walk the dog but there are busy streets on both sides.

Lincoln Park
This park, under the I-54/I-10 interchange, has long grassy areas available for dog-walking. The city has also conducted a long-term mural project on the freeway beams; allowing great access to over a dozen murals.

Marwood Park
Marwood is not a large park but offers access to canals and levees.

Modesto Gomez Park
This park is not very pretty but does have a jogging/walking trail for its entire length that is adequate for a quick jaunt if you are in the neighborhood.

Zaragosa Park
Looks bigger on the city map than it is in reality. Not much of a walk for your dog.

Las Cruces

🐾 **Apodaca Park**
A good place to picnic, a good place to play Frisbee, but a very short walk.

🐾 **Burn Lake**
This park provides a decent dog walking outing around the perimeter of this small lake (more like a pond) where children fish. Worth a quick visit if you're passing by or you live in the neighborhood.

🐾 **Young Park**
Small but pretty, this is a nice park to visit but a very short walk.

Dog Parks

Dog parks often begin as informal gatherings of dog owners that eventaully become legitimized by local government. To date there are no such dog parks in El Paso or Las Cruces. If you do come across a "doggie social hour" in a local park, here are some things to remember:

Tips for enjoying your visit to the dog park

🐾   Keep an eye on your dog and a leash in hand. Situations can change quickly in a dog park.

🐾   Keep puppies younger than 4 months at home until they have all necessary innoculations to allow them to play safely with other dogs. Make certain that your older dog is current on shots and has a valid license.

🐾   ALWAYS clean up after your dog. Failure to pick up your dog's poop is the quickest way to spoil a dog park for every one.

🐾   If your dog begins to play too rough, don't take time to sort out blame - leash the dog and leave immediately.

🐾   Leave your female dog at home if she is in heat.

- Don't volunteer to bring all the dogs in the neighborhood with you when you go. Don't bring any more dogs than you can supervise comfortably.

- Observe and follow all posted regulations at the dogpark.

- **HAVE AS MUCH FUN AS YOUR DOG!**

Index...

Additional Resources

- Creatures, Critters & Crawlers of the Southwest
  by April Kopp

- The Mother Ditch
  by Oliver LaFarge

- Rattlesnakes: Their Habits, Life Histories, & Influence on Mankind
  by Laurence M. Klauber

- Indian Uses of Native Plants
  by Edith Van Allen Murphy

- The Geology of Southern New Mexico: A Beginner's Guide
  by Greg H. Mack

- A Hiking Guide to Doña Ana County, New Mexico
  by Greg S. Magee

♣ <u>Cacti and Succulents of El Paso</u>
      by Clark Champie

♣ <u>Roadside Geology of New Mexico</u>
      by Halka Chronic

♣ <u>Roadside Geology of Texas</u>
      by Darwin Spearing

♣ <u>Chronicles of El Paso</u>
      by Leon Netz

♣ <u>Geology of the Border: Southern New Mexico-</u>
   <u>Northern Chihuahua. El Paso Geological Society</u>
   <u>Field Trip April 10-11, 1981</u>
      by Professor Jerry Hoffer, UTEP Geology
      Department

About The Author

Jessica Powers grew up hiking in the desert tagging along behind her geologist father and even two years of hiking some of the most beautiful trails in the world in New York's Adirondack Mountains couldn't keep her from returning. After meeting her husband Chris while both were members of a street theatre troupe in Melbourne, Australia, she looked forward to the day she could show him the desert around El Paso and southern Mexico. An avid rock-climber until she hurt her wrists, Jessica's outdoor adventures involve mostly footwork these days. Jessica is an editor/publicist for Cinco Puntos Press in El Paso, and has written extensively for the El Paso Scene and Suite 101.com. She loves school and has earned master's degrees in history and writing from the University of Texas at El Paso and New Mexico State University.

Cooper, an energetic yellow lab just entering his teen years, eagerly led Jessica on her exploration of the trails around El Paso and southern New Mexico. He likes nothing better than curling up in the master's bed - unless it is racing up and down desert trails. Cooper is absolutely a dog with a literary pedigree - he is named for James Fenimore Cooper, who most assuredly never hiked an arroyo.

About The Publisher

Cruden Bay Books publishes guidebooks for canine hikers in communities around North America. For more information on A BARK IN THE PARK books please visit our website at **www.hikewithyourdog.com**. At the site you can find:

▸ direct links to more than 2000 dog-friendly parks
▸ dog regulations for national parks in the United States and Canada
▸ recommendations for favorite hikes and can share your favorite hike with your dog with others
▸ beach regulations for dogs on more than 1500 Atlantic Ocean, Pacific Ocean, Gulf of Mexico and Great Lakes beaches
▸ tip sheets for going on a hike with your dog

Cruden Bay Books
PO Box 467
Montchanin, DE 19710
Phone: 302-999-8843
Fax: 302-326-0400
E-mail: crubay@earthlink.net
www.hikewithyourdog.com

Want to order A BARK IN THE PARK books for your organization? Quantity discounts available.